November 1987

Welcome to Des Maines!
With love and Best Wishes in your new home.
Darrell + Jean Hibbs

A TASTE OF TERRACE hill

A collection of pictures,
stories and recipes to give you
a taste of Terrace Hill.

FRONT COVER: Terrace Hill provides the background for a table set with the state china, crystal and silver. Lace cloth was a gift of Ray E. Fowler, Winterset, Iowa. Purchased in Stressa, Italy in 1952, the cloth was entirely hand made by two nuns at the local convent.
Photo by Dave Penney.

Endsheet and chapter page design adapted from the original dance program for the 1869 B.F. Allen Anniversary Party.

TABLE OF CONTENTS

I was overwhelmed by the response to the first and second printings of this cookbook and have been delighted with the lovely new kitchen that we now have because of its success.

It didn't seem right to print more books without updating the pictures of the beautiful new interior of Terrace Hill and adding some new recipes that my friends and I have continued to collect.

Hope you enjoy this new edition of, A Taste of Terrace Hill.

Elegant and stately as it is, Terrace Hill in its 110-year history has never been anything but a home. In many ways, the hub of a home is the kitchen and its activities.

In the very early days, the B. F. Allens christened Terrace Hill with a sparkling gala which set a sumptuous precedent for hospitality and refreshments.

Later, Terrace Hill was the home of the Frederick M. Hubbell family for nearly ninety years. Four generations marked scores of parties, family dinners and special dining occasions.

In 1972 Terrace Hill became the property of the state of Iowa and the home of the Governor. It has been our pleasure to be the first family to reside in this Governor's Mansion and to be a part of the restoration and refurbishing of this great house.

In the five terms during which my husband has been Governor of Iowa, I have had many unforgettable dining experiences. In this book I would like to share some of them with you and also to present recipes collected by many good cooks among my friends and acquaintances.

Billie Ray

Mrs. Robert D. Ray

TERRACE HILL   DES MOINES

Terrace Hill was built by Des Moines banker Benjamin Franklin Allen. It was designed for Allen by noted Chicago architect William W. Boyington. Standing high on a bluff over the Raccoon River, the 20-room rose-colored brick mansion just west of downtown Des Moines was completed in 1869. It was considered a magnificent structure, characterized by many writers as the "finest residence west of the Hudson River." The interior is beautifully designed in walnut, butternut, oak, mahogany and rosewood.

In 1884 the property was sold to F. M. Hubbell. Hubbell, like Allen, was an early Des Moines settler. He was a businessman involved in the development of railroads, real estate, insurance and utility companies. He came to love Terrace Hill as if he had built it himself and several times made major improvements on the house. He raised his family there and lived there until he died.

Terrace Hill was given to the people of Iowa in 1971 by the family of F. M. Hubbell and the legislature later designated it to be used as the official home of our Governors. Renovation and restoration have been designed to return the mansion and grounds to the state of Victorian beauty which once characterized Terrace Hill.

The first floor is being restored to a 19th century appearance. It will serve as the setting for official State functions and a place for Iowans and other visitors to contemplate our history.

The second floor is being refurbished to provide offices for both the Governor and spouse as well as a guest suite for visiting dignitaries. The third floor has been remodeled in contemporary style to serve as the private quarters of the Executive Family.

The music room and drawing room were suited for the most elegant entertaining. The crystal chandeliers, pier mirror, and 17th century tapestry maintain the grandeur of these rooms.

Belter Chair:
This laminated, rosewood, armchair was made about 1855. It is a prime example of work produced by John Henry Belter. Belter held two U.S. patents on his furniture-making processes.

Reception Room:
Originally this room was the library, but served as the Reception Room for the Hubbell family. It was used as a waiting area for callers to this magnificent home.

The sitting room was often the most informal and comfortable room in a Victorian home. However, the elegant furnishings found in more formal rooms were not lacking in the sitting room. The painting is a 19th century copy of Raphael's "Madonna of the Chair." Porcelain figures on the mantle were a gift of the Iowa Antique Association.

The dining room, circa 1890, shows an elaborately stenciled ceiling and two chairs pulled up to the fire. The huge oak sideboard had just been added.

The same room in 1913. The ceiling had been redone in a different design, the chandelier removed and wall sconces added.

Mrs. Ray stands in the recently restored dining room. Gilded plaster work defines the graceful lines of the ceiling. A brass chandelier once again hangs over the table and the shelves over the mantle have been replaced with a mirror. The round table in the breakfast area was used for informal dining.

The rug is an Edward Field rug, woven especially for the room. The original design incorporates the oak tree leaf and the wild rose (the state tree and flower), along with grape vines and leaves, reminiscent of the richly carved wainscoting in the room. The rug was a gift of the Iowa Federation of Women's Clubs.

During the last century, the ornate oak sideboard held many precious posses-sions. Today, silver serving pieces and painted porcelain objects are proudly displayed. The serving pieces, including the magnificent holloware punch bowl, are frequently used for entertaining.

This new spacious and functional kitchen is located on the lower level just below the dining room. It will be used to prepare food for entertaining in the first floor dining room. The Terrace Hill cookbook project made this remodeling possible.

The sitting room was the first room to be decorated. Embroidered silk lampas fabric was reproduced for draperies and for some furniture coverings. Many pieces of furniture came from the estate of Governor Samuel Kirkwood (1860-64, 1876-77).

Sixteen dining room chair seats were needlepointed in the oak leaf and acorn pattern by volunteers.

The graceful silver coffee urn is often used by Mrs. Ray at teas and receptions.

Tables prepared for the New Years Eve celebration, 1980.

GALAS— 1869 and 1979

Benjamin and Arathusa Allen opened Terrace Hill to their friends on January 29, 1869, their fifteenth wedding anniversary. More than 1,000 invitations were mailed, some to New York City. Chicago was represented by at least a dozen guests, including William Boyington, the mansion's architect. Among the Iowa dignitaries attending were Governor Samuel Merrill, Congressman-elect Frank Palmer and judges from the state Supreme Court.

The food was served at 10 p.m. in the dining room. It had been prepared by John Wright, who was brought in from the Opera House Restaurant in Chicago. There were two fruitcakes weighing twenty-five pounds each, ice cream molded in the figure of George Washington, a twenty-five pound lady cake, oysters, boned turkeys in colored jellies and a variety of meats. Flowers were everywhere. The cost for the bouquet at the center of the long dinner table alone was $700.

This gala evening was echoed on June 9, 1979 with an elegant dinner dance sponsored by the Terrace Hill Society, proceeds going toward completion of the restoration. Many of the details of the 1869 Gala were adapted, such as the invitation design and portions of the menu and decor. Following are some photographs and recipes from the 1979 Gala.

Tables draped with flower-sprigged linen bore a sumptuous buffet supper reminiscent of the Gala a century ago.

The Gala was well attended by the Hubbell family, who were joined by the Rays as they gathered on the staircase for the photographer.

1979 GALA MENU

Cold Lobster Mousse in Flaky Pastry Shells
Brie Cheese served with Grapes and Strawberries
★   ★   ★
Turkey Breast garnished with Whole Breast of Turkey en Gelee
Tenderloin of Beef, Sliced
Rack of Lamb garnished with Two Roast Crowns of Lamb
Marinated Vegetables
Potato Nests filled with Peas a la Bonne Femme
★   ★   ★
Decorated Victorian Lady Cakes
Strawberry Tarts
Whole Wheels of Stilton Cheese

LOBSTER MOUSSE TARTLETS

These were passed on silver trays along with glasses of wine as guests arrived at the Gala and strolled around the main floor of Terrace Hill.

Pastry of your choice
4   6 to 7-ounce frozen lobster tails, thawed
¼   cup lemon juice

½   cup butter
3   ounces sherry (dry or cream)
½   teaspoon paprika
Pinch of tarragon
Salt and white pepper to taste

Prepare pastry. (If pie dough is used, fit into miniature muffin pans, prick with fork and bake in 400° oven 5 minutes.)

Bring 2½ quarts of salted water to boil and add lemon juice. Drop in lobster tails and bring back to the boil, reduce heat and barely simmer for 5 minutes. Remove from heat and plunge in cold water.

Cut underskin with kitchen scissors and carefully lift out lobster meat. From the center of each tail, cut six medallions. Reserve.

Put ends in a blender or food processor with butter, sherry, paprika and tarragon. Whirl until slightly fluffy. Salt and pepper to taste. Using pastry tube, fill small shells and top each with a medallion. Makes 24.

CROWN ROAST OF LAMB

The crown roast stood proudly near the end of the buffet table wearing pastel frills to mark its crown shape.

1 **crown roast of lamb consisting of 16 chops (room temperature)**	**Garlic slivers (2 cloves)** ½ **lemon** **Salt and freshly ground black pepper**

A crown roast may be purchased from your butcher by having him tie 2 loins together in a crown shape. Preheat oven to 325°. Insert slivers of garlic into roast with tip of sharp knife. Rub entire crown with lemon and sprinkle with salt and pepper. (Herbs such as rosemary also may be used.) Cover tips of bones with foil to prevent charring.

Roast on rack in open roasting pan about 1 hour 15 minutes or until internal temperature reaches 160° to 165° for slightly rare, or 175° to 180° for well-done. Remove from oven and replace foil with paper frills. Serve immediately on hot platter. Makes 8 servings.

RACK OF LAMB

Each guest watched as the chef carved the rib chop.

1 **whole rack of lamb, about 3 pounds to serve 5 or 6** 2 **tablespoons olive oil** 2 **tablespoons prepared Dijon-type mustard**	1 **cup bread crumbs** 1 **shallot, minced** ¼ **cup chopped fresh parsley** **Salt and pepper** **Clarified unsalted butter**

Have the butcher trim out the large backbone to make slicing and carving easier. Remove as much fat as possible.

Racks of lamb usually consist of 14 chops divided into two racks of seven chops each. Brush olive oil on each half rack. Roast in 400° oven for 15 minutes. Brush the mustard on the meat, then with your hand apply a mixture of the crumbs, shallot, parsley, salt and pepper. Baste with the clarified butter and continue roasting for 35 minutes. Serve with a strong shallot-flavored hollandaise or with mint jelly. Be certain to serve the rack on a very warm platter.

VEGETABLES VINAIGRETTE

Use fresh vegetables cooked to the just-crisp stage, drained and cooled quickly in cold water. Marinate each vegetable separately overnight in refrigerator using the following vinaigrette:

1	tablespoon Dijon-style mustard	¼	teaspoon dried basil
			Salt and pepper to taste
3	tablespoons wine vinegar	2	shallots, finely chopped
3	tablespoons olive oil		(optional)

Whisk ingredients together well. Marinate your choice of vegetables in mixture overnight in refrigerator. Arrange vegetables attractively on large platter.

POTATO NESTS FILLED WITH PEAS A LA BONNE FEMME

Potato Nests may be purchased from specialty stores, or they may be prepared as follows:

Shred potatoes into fine strips on a grater or by using grating blade of food processor. Wash in cold water, dry and use them for lining special wire basket used for this purpose. Trim away any overlapping parts, close basket and plunge into very hot deep oil. Take out of deep-frying pan, turn out, drain and season. Arrange the nest on a napkin and fill with peas a la bonne femme.

Note: Let the wire basket sit in the very hot (450°) oil for a few minutes in order to prevent the potatoes from sticking to the basket. Also, after removing the potato nest from the hot oil, let it sit for a few minutes before trying to remove the nest from the wire basket.

Peas a la Bonne Femme: Melt 1 tablespoon butter in a saucepan and brown lightly 18 small white onions and ¼ pound lean bacon cut in dice and scalded. Remove the onions and the bacon from pan.

Add 2 tablespoons of flour to the butter and cook for a few minutes, stirring with a wooden spoon. Dilute with 1 cup white stock (or canned chicken broth). Boil for 5 minutes. Put 1 quart fresh or frozen garden peas into this sauce, add the small onions and a 4-ounce can of small mushroom caps, drained, into the sauce and add the bacon and a bouquet garni. Simmer for a few minutes with a lid on. Do not let the peas get too well done.

STRAWBERRY TARTS

Probably one of the most talked-about items, everyone was pleasantly startled to find the unexpected taste of chocolate.

Use a short pie dough of your choice	8 ounces chocolate chips
1 quart fresh strawberries	1 jar currant jelly for glaze

Prepare pie dough to fit 8 tart shells. Bake and cool.

Wash and hull fresh strawberries (do not use frozen strawberries). Drain thoroughly and pat each berry dry with paper towels. Berries may be used whole or sliced in half, reserving 8 whole berries for garnish.

Melt chocolate chips in top of double boiler. With a pastry brush or small spatula, glaze the inside of the tart shells with the chocolate. Place on cookie sheet and place in refrigerator no longer than 20 minutes to cool.

When shells with chocolate glaze are cool, place berries in shells. Glaze with currant jelly. Garnish top with a whole strawberry. Whipped cream may be passed or tubed around the whole strawberry. Makes 8 tarts.

LADY CAKE

Made into Petits Fours, these alternated with the tarts to make a beautiful tiered dessert presentation.

1¾ cups cake flour	1 teaspoon almond extract
2 teaspoons baking powder	Grated rind of 1 lemon
1 cup sugar	3 egg whites
¾ cup butter	Confectioners' sugar
½ cup milk	

Preheat oven to 350°. Have all ingredients at room temperature. Sift cake flour before measuring, then resift twice with baking powder. Set aside. Sift sugar and set aside. Cream butter until soft; add sugar gradually, creaming until very light, about 5 to 8 minutes. Add the flour mixture in 3 parts to the butter mixture alternately with milk. Stir batter for a few minutes after each addition. Add almond extract and lemon rind. Whip egg whites until stiff but not dry. Fold lightly into batter.   Continued. . . .

Bake in greased 9-inch tube pan, about 45 minutes. Sprinkle with confectioners' sugar or spread when cool with the following icing:

Icing: Blend well 2 cups confectioners' sugar with ¼ cup soft butter. Beat in 1 or more teaspoons cream. Add grated rind and juice of 1 lemon or orange, or 3 tablespoons of liqueur such as apricot or creme de cacao.

Instead of baking cake in tube pan it may be baked in a loaf pan or in a rectangular pan for making into Petits Fours. For these, cut into serving pieces and ice top and sides, decorating as desired.

DECORATING FOOD FOR A BUFFET

Almost every elegant professionally-done buffet features one or more showpiece platters of artistically decorated food. (See picture of turkey for Gala on p. 14). Often it is a whole baked salmon or a whole roast turkey or ham painted with what looks like white enamel and then decorated with leaves and flowers made of vegetables, fruits and eggs. Meat or seafood molds are also good to decorate. All such food decorations must be edible and are glazed with a consomme gelatin which acts as a preservative and adds additional flavor.

Food decorating involves two basic substances, jellied consomme (Gelee) to provide a protective coating and to make the decorations stick; and Chaud-Froid (jellied white sauce) to provide the beautiful white surface on which to put the decorations.

While not exactly a last-minute project, if enough time and patience are allowed, food decorating is not as difficult as it looks and certainly will create a stir at your next buffet. Suggestion: invite an interested friend or two to join you for the decorating. A little camaraderie adds to the fun, bolsters your courage and makes the results even more rewarding.

Food to be decorated should be cooked or made the day before and refrigerated until decorating. Our testers had fun with this. Their experience was with the Mousse Jambon (p. 65) and Eggs Stuffed with Caviar (p. 61).

JELLIED CONSOMME (GELEE)

Gelee, since it holds foods together, must be stiffer than the ordinary cold jellied consomme which is contained by a serving cup.

2	packages unflavored gelatin	½	teaspoon dry tarragon leaves
½	cup cold water	1	carrot, minced
4	egg whites	1	small leek or 2 green onions
4½	cups cold chicken stock	2	tablespoons chopped parsley
1	teaspoon salt	2	tablespoons Port
Freshly-ground pepper to taste		1	tablespoon Cognac

Put gelatin, cold water and egg whites into saucepan. Beat to a froth. Add cold chicken stock, salt, pepper, tarragon and carrot. Clean leek and slice thin, using 2 inches of the green tops. Add leek and parsley.

Stir-cook over medium heat until starting to boil. Immediately reduce heat to a simmer and stop stirring. Under no conditions let this boil or the impurities will boil back into the consomme as fast as they collect. Simmer for about 15 minutes.

Rinse a clean linen cloth in cold water. Line a strainer with the cloth and set over a porcelain or crockery bowl. When Gelee is done, carefully pour liquid through a hole in the cooked egg whites, being careful not to disturb the coagulated whites, and into the cloth-lined strainer. Cool Gelee, then add Port and Cognac.

If Gelee is to be used immediately, pour some into a small stainless-steel pan or bowl. Set into a dish filled with ice cubes and water. Stir with a paint brush until it starts to thicken. Remove from ice and use the glaze. If Gelee becomes too thick, heat to melt it and then cool again in ice water.

Gelee can be used to coat seafood molds, cold chicken, stuffed eggs and cold meats.

JELLIED WHITE SAUCE (CHAUD-FROID)

"Chaud-Froid" means hot-cold. It is made by adding gelatin to a hot Bechamel sauce, then cooling and painting onto various prepared foods, such as whole baked salmon, turkey breast and baked ham. The white glaze of Chaud-Froid makes a perfect background for colorful food decorations.

1 tablespoon unflavored gelatin	Celery tops from 3 branches
½ cup sherry	¼ cup butter
2 cups milk	¼ cup flour
2 sliced shallots	½ teaspoon salt
3 sprigs parsley	½ teaspoon sugar
	½ cup whipping cream

Soak gelatin in sherry. Put 1 cup milk into a pan. Add shallots, parsley and celery tops. Bring to a boil and then remove from heat, cover, and let stand. Melt butter in saucepan. Add flour, salt and sugar. Stir-cook for about 2 minutes. Remove from heat. Add remaining cup of cold milk and the whipping cream. Strain the hot milk into the saucepan. Heat and stir until thickened.

When thick, add soaked gelatin and stir until dissolved. Set pan in ice water. Stir until mixture starts to set and then use to coat cold cooked foods. If sauce sets too much, reheat and chill again to the proper consistency.

To decorate on Chaud-Froid: Prepare and chill food which is to be decorated. Coat object with Chaud-Froid, either by painting on with a soft paint brush or by spooning sauce over. (Place object on rack to catch extra sauce and reuse.) Give object two coats of Chaud-Froid, chilling slightly after each coat. Make decorations as described below. Dip in Gelee (jellied consomme) and arrange on white coating in desired pattern. Use tweezers, toothpick or point of sharp knife to set decorations in place. When food is decorated, brush entire piece including decorations with a coat of Gelee. Refrigerate until set (about an hour), then give the food a second coat of Gelee. This second coat will keep the decorations from drying out and will give the piece a fine, professional appearance.

HOW TO MAKE DECORATIONS

Have your design in mind before you begin. Have a shallow pan of Gelee handy. As you make parts of the decorations, let them lie in the Gelee and push them around with a knife or toothpick until you see the pattern you want. Make more pieces than you need so you can pick out just the right ones.

Leaves and Stems: To use green-onion tops, split hollow tops. Drop into boiling water, then into cold water. (Blanching makes them greener.) Lay on paper towel. Cut into stems or leaf shapes. To use cucumber, remove green skin in wide strips with a potato peeler. Place on cutting board and with sharp knife cut into desired shapes.

Flower Pots: Cut a 1/16-inch-thick lengthwise slice from a cooked carrot. Then cut out a flower pot from the widest part of the slice. Put pot into brown coloring made by mixing brown gravy sauce with water. Let stand until pot is desired color. Blot on paper towels. Run green onion stems out of pot and top the stems with assorted food flowers.

Jonquils: Cut a ½-inch piece from the bottom of a cooked carrot. Trim it to a cylinder about ¼ inch in diameter. Hollow out the center with the point of a knife, then taper the outside down to the bottom. Make V cuts around the top. Place this jonquil center at the end of a stem. Cut petals from a thin slice of carrot by cutting triangular pieces and notching one side.

Black-eyed Susans: Cut petals from thin slice of cooked carrot. Make center from the tip of a black olive.

Tulips: Cut circles from a lengthwise slice of cooked carrot. Make two V cuts from one side to make the circle look like a tulip.

Holly: Cut leaves from green pepper, tiny circles from red pepper. (Circles can be cut with end of a 1/16-inch pastry tube.)

Poinsettia: Cut elongated petals from a shiny red pepper and place around a center of sieved hard-cooked egg yolk. Make green pepper leaves.

BRUNCHES,
COFFEES,
AND TEAS

SANTA FE FRENCH TOAST

This is the famous breakfast served in the heyday of the Santa Fe railroad aboard the Santa Fe Chief.

8   eggs
4   tablespoons half and half
1   teaspoon vanilla
½   teaspoon salt
4   1-inch bread slices, trimmed

Beat together the eggs, half and half and vanilla. Add the salt. Place bread in pan and soak overnight in egg mixture. Quick fry in deep fat until golden brown. Place on cookie sheet and bake at 350° for 10 minutes. Serve with syrup, jam or confectioners' sugar. Makes 4 servings.

EGGS ORIENTALE

Exotic fare for brunch or lunch.

8   hard-cooked eggs
1½   tablespoons anchovy paste
2   tablespoons mayonnaise
6   ripe olives, chopped
1   tablespoon lemon juice
2   tablespoons chopped walnuts or pecans
3   tablespoons butter or margarine, melted
3   tablespoons flour
1½   cups milk or chicken broth
Salt and pepper
1   tablespoon Worcestershire sauce
1½   cups cooked and coarsely chopped shrimp (optional)
½   pound sliced mushrooms, lightly sauteed

Cut the eggs in half lengthwise. Remove the yolks and mash. Mix the yolks with the anchovy paste, mayonnaise, olives, lemon juice and nuts. Fill the egg whites with this mixture and lay the stuffed eggs in a shallow buttered casserole or pie plate. Make a cream sauce with the butter, flour, and milk or chicken broth. Season to taste and add the Worcestershire sauce. Stir in shrimp and mushrooms and pour over the eggs. Bake 15 minutes in 325° oven. May be served as is or with green spinach noodles. Serves 8.

HAM AND EGG BRUNCH

6 eggs, hard-cooked and
  chopped
3 tablespoons butter or
  margarine
3 tablespoons flour
1 teaspoon dry mustard
¾ teaspoon salt
1/8 teaspoon pepper
1½ cups milk

1 teaspoon horseradish
1 tablespoon Worcestershire
  sauce
1 tablespoon chili sauce
Dash tabasco
2 cups diced ham
½ cup sliced ripe olives
¾ cup sharp Cheddar cheese,
  grated

Melt butter, stir in flour, mustard, salt, pepper and milk. Stir and cook over medium heat until thickened. Stir in horseradish, Worcestershire sauce, chili sauce, tabasco and cheese.

In 1½-quart casserole, arrange in layers the ham, eggs, olives and cheese sauce. Bake in 350° oven 30 minutes. Serve with toasted English muffins. Makes 8 servings.

MONTEREY SOUFFLE

A light casserole for brunch or lunch.

2 cups grated Monterey Jack
  cheese
2 cups grated Cheddar cheese
2 4-ounce cans green chilies,
  drained and diced

4 eggs, separated
⅔ cup evaporated milk
1 tablespoon flour
1 teaspoon salt
¼ teaspoon pepper
2 medium tomatoes, sliced

Combine cheese and chilies and place in well-greased 13x9x2-inch casserole. Beat egg whites until stiff peaks form. In another bowl, combine beaten egg yolks, milk, flour and seasonings. Fold egg whites into egg yolk mixture and pour over cheeses. Use a fork to swirl egg mixture into cheese. Bake in 325° oven 25 minutes. Remove from oven and cover top with sliced tomatoes. Bake another 25 minutes or until a silver knife comes out clean. Makes 8 servings.

BACON-EGG CASSEROLE

A crunchy eye-opener.

2 tablespoons butter or margarine	1½ cups shredded process American or Cheddar cheese
½ cup chopped onion	1½ teaspoons dry mustard
2 tablespoons flour	6 hard-cooked eggs
1½ cups milk	15 to 20 slices bacon, crisp-cooked and crumbled
	2 cups crushed potato chips

Melt butter in saucepan and saute onion until yellow. Add flour and stir; slowly add milk. Cook and stir until thickened and bubbly. Add cheese and mustard and stir until smooth. Remove from heat. In buttered 1½-quart casserole, layer 3 eggs, sliced, half of sauce, half of crumbled bacon and half of crushed chips. Repeat with remaining ingredients. Bake in 350° oven 15 to 20 minutes. May be made and refrigerated a day ahead. If chilled, add 10 minutes baking time. Makes 6 servings.

COUNTRY BRUNCH

The flavor depends on the sausage. Make sure you use the kind you particularly like.

9 slices bread, cubed	8 eggs
2½ pounds bulk sausage, sauteed and drained	3 cups milk
10 ounces Cheddar cheese, grated	1½ teaspoons dry mustard
	½ teaspoon salt
	¼ teaspoon pepper

Place half of bread cubes in bottom of 13x9x2-inch pan. Put half of sausage on top, followed by half of cheese. Repeat layers. Beat eggs with milk, mustard, salt and pepper. Pour mixture over layers in pan. Cover and refrigerate overnight. Remove cover and bake in 350° oven 1 hour. Makes 12 to 14 servings.

BRUNCH BUFFET

This make-ahead casserole is ideally suited for large scale morning entertaining.

1½ pounds fresh mush-rooms or 3 8-ounce cans button mushrooms, drained	3 pounds cooked ham, cubed
	2 cups packaged stuffing mix
3 dozen hard-cooked eggs, deviled	2 cups grated process American cheese

Line 2-13 x 9 x 2-inch casseroles with eggs, face up; lay ham and mushrooms on top of eggs. Pour Cream Sauce over ham, mushrooms and eggs. Mix cheese and stuffing mix together and sprinkle over top. Bake in 350° oven for 30 to 45 minutes or until sauce is bubbly. Make the day before using and refrigerate. Makes 20 to 24 servings.

Cream Sauce: Melt ½ pound butter and add 1 cup flour, stirring constantly. Slowly pour in 2¼ quarts milk, continuing to stir. Add 2 teaspoons salt and ½ teaspoon white pepper. Cook on low heat, stirring frequently until thickened.

BACON-HAM BAKE

Delightful flavor neatly wrapped for brunch or lunch.

8 strips bacon, uncooked	Dijon mustard
4 ham slices, ½-inch thick	4 pineapple rings
	4 cherry tomatoes, optional

Crisscross two bacon strips and place a slice of ham in the center. Spread ham with mustard and top with pineapple ring. Pull bacon over all and secure with toothpick.

Bake in a 400° oven for 40 minutes or until bacon is very crisp. Top with a cherry tomato before serving. Makes 4 servings.

BASIC FRENCH OMELET

With an assortment of fillings and the right kind of kitchen, the making of individual omelets can be the entertainment as well as the food.

2 eggs	Salt, pepper, desired herbs
1 tablespoon water	1 tablespoon butter
	Desired filling

Beat eggs with water, just to combine. Do not overbeat. Season as you like.

Heat butter in omelet pan, just until foam begins to subside and butter takes on a very light brown color. Quickly turn egg mixture into pan all at once and immediately shake pan vigorously (as you would for popped corn).

After about 45 seconds of cooking, slide egg mixture toward edge of pan which is opposite to handle. Spoon filling on omelet, keeping filling away from edges of omelet. Slide omelet to edge of pan. Grasp handle with up-turned fist-like grip. Flip over onto warmed plate and serve immediately.

To hold an omelet: Undercook omelet slightly, fill and turn onto plate as usual. Quickly slit top and dot with butter. Keep in warm oven.

Onion-Bacon Filling for Omelet: Cook 4 to 6 slices bacon until crisp. Remove and set aside. Pour off all but 3 tablespoons bacon drippings. Saute 3 medium onions, sliced, in bacon drippings. When onions have been sauteed, crumble bacon and add. Makes filling for 2 to 3 omelets.

Provencale-Style Filling for Omelet: Saute ½ onion, sliced; ½ tomato, sliced; 4 to 6 mushrooms, sliced; and 2 tablespoons slivered green onion in 2 tablespoons olive oil. Peel and slice 1 small eggplant. Using fingers or brush, coat both sides of eggplant slices with olive oil. Place on baking sheet and bake in 400° oven about 30 minutes or until nicely browned. Remove to cutting board and cut into small dice. Add to onion mixture. Add oregano, rosemary, minced parsley, salt and pepper to taste. Keep warm (or reheat, if done ahead) while preparing omelet. Makes filling for 3 to 4 omelets.

On August 7, 1869, Terrace Hill was opened to give astronomers a vantage point from which to view a total eclipse of the sun.

PRUNE KUCHEN

½ cup butter, softened
1 cup all-purpose flour
2 tablespoons sugar
¼ teaspoon baking powder
¼ teaspoon salt

2 cups pitted dried prunes, chopped
½ cup plus 2 tablespoons sugar
2 egg yolks
1 cup sour cream
1 teaspoon ground cinnamon

Blend butter, flour, 2 tablespoons sugar, baking powder and salt. Pat over bottom and up sides of 8x8x2-inch baking pan. Mix prunes with remaining sugar. Place over pastry and bake in a 350° oven 15 minutes.

Beat together egg yolks, sour cream and cinnamon. Pour over prunes and bake another 30 minutes. Let cool before cutting. Makes 16 2-inch squares to eat with fingers or 12 larger slices to serve on a plate with a dollop of whipped cream.

DANISH PUFF

Quick, easy and simply delicious.

½ cup butter or margarine
1 cup sifted all-purpose flour
2 tablespoons water
½ cup butter or margarine
1 cup water

1 teaspoon almond flavoring
1 cup sifted all-purpose flour
3 eggs
Confectioners' Sugar Icing
Chopped nuts, optional

Cut ½ cup butter into 1 cup flour. Sprinkle with 2 tablespoons water and mix with fork. Form into ball; divide in half. Pat dough into two 12x3-inch strips 3 inches apart on ungreased cookie sheet.

Place ½ cup butter and 1 cup water in saucepan; bring to a rolling boil. Remove from heat and add almond flavoring. Stir gradually into 1 cup flour, stirring briskly to keep from lumping. When smooth and thick, add eggs, one at a time, and beat until smooth. Divide in half and spread one half evenly over each piece of pastry. Bake in 350° oven 50 minutes or until topping is crisp and browned. Frost with Confectioners' Sugar Icing. Serve hot or cold. Makes 12 to 14 servings.

Confectioner's Sugar Icing: Melt ⅓ cup butter or margarine in saucepan. Blend in 2 cups confectioners' sugar and 1 teaspoon almond flavoring. Stir in 2 to 4 tablespoons water, one tablespoon at a time, until icing is of spreading consistency. Sprinkle with chopped nuts.

PEANUT BUBBLE RING

1	loaf frozen bread dough	1	4½-ounce package salted
1	4-ounce package regular		peanuts, chopped
	butterscotch pudding mix	1	teaspoon ground cinnamon
½	cup packed brown sugar	4	tablespoons butter or
			margarine, melted

Thaw bread dough in refrigerator overnight. Quarter loaf lengthwise; cut each quarter into 8 cubes (32 cubes in all). Combine dry pudding mix, brown sugar, peanuts and cinnamon. Dip each dough cube in melted butter and roll in pudding mixture. Place in greased 6-cup ring mold in 3 layers. Drizzle with any remaining butter and sprinkle with any remaining pudding mixture. Cover; let rise in warm place till nearly double, 1 to 1¼ hours. Bake in 350° oven 20 to 25 minutes. Let stand in pan 2 minutes before inverting onto rack to cool. Makes 10 servings.

COFFEE CAKE EXCEPTIONALE

This moist, quick bread will become a favorite once tried.

¾	cup soft butter or margarine	1½	teaspoons baking powder
1½	cups sugar	1½	teaspoons baking soda
3	eggs	¼	teaspoon salt
1½	teaspoons vanilla	1½	cups dairy sour cream
3	cups all-purpose flour		Cinnamon-Nut Filling
			(below)

Heat oven to 350°. Grease a tube pan, 10x4 inches or two loaf pans, 9x5x3 inches. Cream butter and sugar thoroughly; beat in eggs and vanilla. Stir flour, baking powder, soda and salt together; mix into creamed mixture alternately with the sour cream. For tube pan spread ⅓ of batter into pan. Sprinkle with ⅓ of filling. Repeat twice. For loaf pan spread ¼ of batter into each pan. Sprinkle each with ¼ of filling. Repeat. Bake 50 to 60 minutes. Cool slightly in pan(s) before removing. Makes 1 round coffee cake or 2 loaves.

Cinnamon-nut filling: Stir together ½ cup packed brown sugar, ½ cup chopped nuts and 1½ teaspoons ground cinnamon.

BOHEMIAN COFFEE CAKE

1 cup cooking oil	1 teaspoon cinnamon
1 cup brown sugar, packed	1 teaspoon nutmeg
1 cup granulated sugar	1 teaspoon vanilla
1 cup buttermilk	2½ cups flour
1 cup flaked coconut	2 eggs
1 teaspoon salt	1 cup pecans
1 teaspoon soda	Cream Cheese Frosting
	Slivered almonds, optional

Mix all ingredients together in order given and pour into a greased and floured tube pan. Bake in 350° oven for one hour. Makes 14 to 16 servings.

Cream Cheese Frosting: Mix together 1 8-ounce package cream cheese, softened; 1 pound confectioners' sugar, ½ cup butter or margarine, softened and 2 teaspoons almond extract. Frost cake when cool and decorate top with slivered almonds, if desired.

ANGEL SANDWICHES

1 cup shortening (half butter or margarine)	1½ cups cut-up dates
	1½ cups raisins
1 cup confectioners' sugar	¼ cup sugar
2 cups flour	1½ cups water
	Sweetened Whipped Cream Topping

Heat oven to 350°. Mix shortening and confectioners' sugar thoroughly. Measure flour by dipping method or by sifting. Stir flour into shortening mixture. Press and flatten with hand to cover bottom of ungreased 13x9x2-inch pan. Bake 20 minutes. Blend fruit, sugar and water in saucepan. Cook over low heat, stirring constantly, until thickened, about 10 minutes. Cool both crust and filling. Spread filling over crust and spread Topping over filling. Chill before cutting. Store covered in refrigerator. Makes about 8 dozen 1″ squares.

Sweetened Whipped Cream Topping.—Beat 1 cup chilled whipping cream, ¼ cup sifted confectioners' sugar and ¼ teaspoon vanilla until stiff.

EUROPEAN EASTER BREAD

A deliciously rich sweet yeast bread traditionally used only for very special holiday occasions.

1 cake yeast or 1 package active dry yeast	½ teaspoon salt
¼ cup warm water	1 lemon, juice and rind
2 tablespoons flour	1 teaspoon vanilla
1 teaspoon sugar	10 large eggs
1 cup milk	10 to 12 cups all-purpose flour
½ cup butter	1 egg
3 cups sugar	¼ cup milk
	Colored sugar

Dissolve yeast in warm water with 2 tablespoons flour and 1 teaspoon sugar. Let rise (5 minutes). Place in saucepan milk, butter, sugar, salt, lemon juice and rind. Heat and stir until mixture is nearly boiling, but do not boil. Let cool; add vanilla.

Beat 10 eggs until thick. Add flour and yeast mixture alternately with butter mixture. When firm enough to handle, start pushing dough together with hands. Turn out on floured board and knead, adding flour and kneading thoroughly until dough is smooth and elastic.

Oil large bowl. Place dough in bowl and turn once to oil top side. Cover with towel. Place in warm place to rise—3 to 4 hours. Punch down, let rise again another 3 to 4 hours.

Oil board and hands. Divide dough into 3 portions. Working with 1 portion at a time, cut each into 3 pieces. Roll each piece between hands to elongate. Braid 3 pieces together and place in greased 9x5x3-inch loaf pan. Repeat with remaining two-thirds of dough.

Let rise again until doubled. Beat 1 egg with ¼ cup milk. Brush top of loaves and sprinkle with colored sugar. Bake at very low heat in 200° oven about 1 hour until tops are lightly browned and crusty and pick comes out of center clean. Cool. Remove from pans. Makes 3 large loaves. Freezes well and stores 2 weeks in refrigerator. Serve warm or cold, plain or with butter.

CINNAMON TWISTS

1 cup sour cream	1 teaspoon sugar
3 tablespoons sugar	2 eggs, slightly beaten
3 tablespoons butter or margarine	3½ cups all-purpose flour
1/8 teaspoon baking soda	¼ cup butter or margarine, melted
½ teaspoon salt	6 tablespoons packed brown sugar
1 package active dry yeast	
½ cup warm water	1½ teaspoons ground cinnamon

Bring sour cream, sugar, butter and baking soda to a boil. Remove from heat and cool to luke warm. Add salt. Soften yeast in water and sugar; add to cream mixture. Add eggs and flour; form ball (dough will be sticky). Cover and let stand 5 minutes.

On floured board, roll dough (sprinkled with flour) to 24x9-inch rectangle. Spread with mixture of melted butter, brown sugar and cinnamon. Roll jelly roll fashion. Cut in 24 1-inch slices. Twist and place on greased cookie sheet. Let rise 1½ hours. Bake in 375° oven 15 minutes. Cool and frost with powdered sugar icing.

Vanilla Icing: Combine 2 tablespoons butter or margarine, 2 cups confectioners' sugar, 1 teaspoon vanilla, 3 tablespoons milk and a dash of salt. Sprinkle with chopped nuts, if desired.

TEATIME LEMON BREAD

1½ cups flour	½ cup milk
1 teaspoon baking powder	2 teaspoons grated lemon rind
1 teaspoon salt	3 tablespoons lemon juice
⅓ cup butter, softened	½ cup chopped nuts
1 cup sugar	Lemon Sugar Syrup
2 eggs	

Stir together flour, baking powder and salt. Cream together butter and sugar until fluffy; beat in eggs. Add flour alternately with milk. Stir in lemon peel, juice and nuts. Pour into a greased and floured 8½x4½x2½-inch pan. Bake in 350° oven 1 hour. Cool cake on rack 10 minutes; turn out. Brush Lemon Sugar Syrup on top and sides of cake slowly. Let stand 24 hours before cutting.

Lemon Sugar Syrup: Combine 3 tablespoons lemon juice and ½ cup sugar in small bowl. (Sugar does not have to be dissolved.)

COCONUT DATE BARS

½ cup butter or margarine,
   softened
½ cup confectioners' sugar
1 cup plus 2 tablespoons flour
2 eggs
1 cup firmly packed brown
   sugar

1 teaspoon baking powder
1⅓ cup flaked coconut
½ cup chopped pitted dates
   or chopped raisins
½ teaspoon vanilla

In small bowl of mixer, cream butter. Gradually stir in confectioners' sugar. Stir in the 1 cup flour. Spread evenly in bottom of ungreased 9x9x2-inch pan. Bake in 350° oven 15 minues. Meanwhile, in large bowl beat eggs until frothy. Gradually add brown sugar beating until light and fluffy. Stir in the 2 tablespoons flour and the baking powder. Stir in coconut, dates and vanilla. Pour over baked mixture in pan. Spread smooth. Continue baking about 30 minutes longer. Cool in pan. Cut into bars. Makes 18 bars.

RAGELACH PASTRIES

A not-too-sweet confection best served fresh but may be frozen.

1 cup butter or margarine,
   softened
8 ounces cream cheese,
   softened

2 cups sifted all-purpose flour
¼ teaspoon salt
1 cup chopped walnuts
½ cup sugar
1 teaspoon ground cinnamon

Combine butter and cheese until blended. Mix in flour and salt. Shape into 14 balls. Chill overnight.

Roll each ball into 6 inch circle. Cut into quarters. Combine nuts, sugar and cinnamon. Drop a teaspoon sugar mixture on each quarter. Spread over surface. Roll up, starting at wide edge.

Place, point side down, on ungreased cookie sheet. Bake in 350° oven 15 minutes or until light brown. Makes 5 dozen.

OLD ENGLISH SPICE BARS

1½ cups raisins	2 eggs
2 cups water	3 cups all-purpose flour
1 cup shortening	1½ teaspoons baking soda
1½ cups sugar	1 teaspoon ground cinnamon
1 teaspoon vanilla	½ teaspoon salt

Cook raisins in water until plumped. Drain, reserving 1 cup liquid. Beat together shortening and sugar until light and fluffy. Beat in eggs and vanilla. Sift together dry ingredients. Add to creamed mixture alternately with raisin liquid. Stir in raisins.

Spread in greased and floured 15x10x1-inch baking pan. Bake in 350° oven 25 minutes. Frost with confectioners' sugar frosting, if desired. Makes about 6 dozen 2x1-inch bars.

QUICK APRICOT PASTRIES

These tasty pastries are so easy and quick that you will want to keep the ingredients on hand for frequent use.

1 package refrigerated crescent rolls	1 beaten egg
	1 tablespoon sugar
½ cup apricot jam	½ teaspoon vanilla
1 cup dairy sour cream	

Unroll crescent rolls; pat into bottom of buttered 13x9x2-inch baking dish. Spread with jam. Bake at 425° for 15 minutes; remove from oven. Reduce heat to 325°. Combine remaining ingredients. Pour evenly over rolls; return to oven. Bake 5 to 6 minutes more. Serve warm. Makes 9 servings.

DIAMOND SHORTBREAD CRISPS

1 cup butter	1 egg yolk
1 cup sugar	2 cups all-purpose flour
1 teaspoon vanilla	1 beaten egg white
½ teaspoon ground cinnamon	½ cup chopped nuts
¼ teaspoon salt	

Cream together butter, sugar, vanilla, cinnamon and salt until light and fluffy. Blend in egg yolk, then flour. Press thinly on a large, greased cookie sheet. Spread with egg white. Sprinkle with nuts. Bake in 275° oven 1 hour. Cut into diamonds immediately. Makes about 3 dozen.

ORANGE NUT BREAD

2 tablespoons shortening	2 cups all-purpose flour
1 cup sugar	1 teaspoon baking powder
1 egg	½ teaspoon baking soda
2 oranges	½ teaspoon salt
	1 cup chopped pecans

Cream shortening and sugar. Add egg. Grate oranges. Squeeze oranges; add enough water to juice to make 1 cup. Add orange peel to juice.

Sift dry ingredients and add to creamed mixture alternately with orange juice mixture. Stir in nuts. Spread in a greased and floured 8½x4½x2½-inch loaf pan. Bake in 350° oven 1 hour.

MARMALADE BREAD

The marmalade is already on the bread.

3 cups sifted all-purpose flour	1 beaten egg
3 teaspoons baking powder	¾ cup orange juice
1 teaspoon salt	¼ cup salad oil or melted
¼ teaspoon baking soda	shortening
1 1-pound jar (1½ cups)	1 cup coarsely chopped walnuts
orange marmalade	

Sift together dry ingredients. Reserve ¼ cup of the marmalade. Combine remaining 1¼ cups marmalade, egg, orange juice and salad oil. Add to flour mixture, stirring just until moistened. Stir in nuts.

Turn into a greased 9x5x3-inch loaf pan. Bake in 350° oven 1 hour. Remove bread from pan. Place on cookie sheet. Spread top with reserved marmalade. Return to oven about one minute or until glazed. Cool on rack.

CRANBERRY MUFFINS

Great accompaniment for turkey.

2 cups flour	2 cups whole cranberries
2 teaspoons baking powder	1 cup milk
1 cup sugar	3 tablespoons melted butter or
½ teaspoon salt	margarine

Mix first four ingredients together. Add cranberries, milk and melted butter. Mix well. Pour into greased muffin cups and bake in 375° oven for 30 minutes. Makes 18 muffins.

Sauce: Add ½ cup butter, 1 cup sugar and ¾ cup whipping cream together in saucepan and bring just to a boil. Reduce heat and cook one minute. Spoon over cooled muffins.

SPICE BREAD

Enough reason to have a brunch or a coffee.

1 cup sugar	1 teaspoon ground cinnamon
½ cup butter or margarine, softened	½ teaspoon ground allspice
	½ teaspoon ground nutmeg
1 egg	½ teaspoon salt
1 cup seedless raisins	2 cups all purpose flour
1 cup sweetened applesauce	1 teaspoon baking soda
½ cup chopped walnuts	2 tablespoons hot water

Blend sugar, margarine and egg thoroughly. Add raisins, applesauce and walnuts. Sift the spices and salt with flour and add in several additions. Before the last addition, stir in baking soda dissolved in hot water. Beat well.

Pour into 2 greased 8½x4½x2½-inch loaf pans. Bake in 350° oven for 1 hour. (Keeps well in freezer.)

On October 12, 1869, B. F. Allen was elected to the Iowa Senate. Soon after that, he gave a party at Terrace Hill to electioneer the building of a new Capitol.

BANANA BREAD

A delightfully light-textured bread.

½ cup butter or margarine	2 cups sifted all-purpose flour
1 cup sugar	1½ teaspoons baking powder
2 eggs	¾ teaspoon baking soda
1½ cups mashed bananas	½ teaspoon salt
1 teaspoon lemon juice	¼ cup dairy sour cream
	½ cup chopped walnuts

Cream together butter and sugar. Add eggs, one at a time, beating well after each addition. Combine bananas and lemon juice; add to sugar mixture. Beat well. Sift together dry ingredients. Add to creamed mixture alternately with sour cream. Fold in nuts. Pour in two 9x5x3-inch loaf pans. Bake in 375° oven 35 to 45 minutes. Makes 2 loaves.

ZUCCHINI BREAD

3 eggs	3 cups sifted all-purpose flour
1 cup cooking oil	1 teaspoon baking soda
2 cups sugar	1 teaspoon salt
2 cups grated zucchini	½ teaspoon baking powder
2 teaspoons vanilla	1 teaspoon ground cinnamon
	½ cup chopped nuts

Beat eggs; stir in oil, sugar, zucchini and vanilla. Sift together flour, baking soda, baking powder, salt and cinnamon. Stir into egg mixture. Fold in nuts. Pour into two greased 8½x4½x2½-inch loaf pans. Bake in 325° oven 1 hour and 15 minutes or until toothpick inserted comes out clean. Makes 2 loaves.

People often came to Terrace Hill in its early days to buy flowers from the hothouse.

luncheons

CHILLED CUCUMBER SOUP

The coldest thing we can think of on a hot summer evening.

1 cup chicken broth	Dash white pepper
2½ cups peeled, seeded,	4 drops tabasco sauce
chopped cucumber	Juice from ½ lemon
1 teaspoon salt	1 cup sour cream

In blender, blend chicken broth and cucumbers. Season with salt, pepper, Tabasco sauce and lemon juice. Put blender on high for 2 minutes. Add sour cream. Blend 2 more minutes at high speed. Test for flavor. Chill thoroughly before serving. Top with ½ cup of finely diced unpeeled cucumber as garnish. Makes 4 cups.

GAZPACHO

3 cups tomato juice	1 small cucumber, chopped
2 tablespoons olive oil	1 small green pepper, chopped
2 tablespoons wine vinegar	3 stalks celery, chopped
1 clove garlic, cut up	¼ medium onion, chopped
2 tomatoes, peeled and	4 sprigs parsley
quartered	1 slice bread, torn
¼ teaspoon pepper	Toasted croutons

Blend ingredients together in blender, dividing all in half if blender will not hold entire contents. Let stand an hour or so in refrigerator to blend flavors. Serve in mugs or bowls, garnished with croutons, if desired. Makes 6 to 8 servings.

F. M. Hubbell and his wife Frances signed the deed to Terrace Hill on May 9, 1884. They paid Allen $20,000 down and the remaining $40,000 within ten years. The 1885 census showed the residents as F. M. and Frances Hubbell, children Frederick, Beulah, and Grover, plus three female domestics and three male laborers.

CREAM OF ASPARAGUS SOUP

1	pound fresh cut asparagus	⅓	cup minced onion
6	cups chicken broth, or 3 13¾-ounce cans chicken broth	3	tablespoons butter or margarine
½	teaspoon salt	¼	cup flour
		2	egg yolks
		½	cup whipping cream

Cook asparagus in boiling chicken broth with salt until tender. Drain, reserving broth. Meanwhile, cook onion in butter until soft. Blend in flour and stir until bubbly. Blend in chicken broth. Bring to boiling. Reduce heat and simmer 5 minutes. Add asparagus and puree mixture in blender until smooth. Blend egg yolks and cream in bowl. Add 1 cup of hot soup to egg yolk mixture. Beat into remaining soup gradually. Return to heat but do not boil. Makes 6 to 8 servings.

BROCCOLI SOUP

Rich, creamy soup. Serve with bread and salad and lunch is ready. Excellent served cold as first course for dinner.

1	package frozen chopped broccoli	1	cup sour cream
1	medium onion, chopped	1	10¾-ounce can cream of mushroom soup
1	teaspoon nutmeg	2	tablespoons butter or margarine
1	cup chicken broth		

Cook the broccoli, onion, nutmeg and chicken broth for six minutes. Place in blender or food processor and add the sour cream, mushroom soup, and butter. Blend on high for 20 seconds. Return to heat before serving; do not boil. Makes 6 servings.

LEMON LENTIL SOUP

A thick, flavorful soup that improves with age.

1 **pound dried lentils**	2½ **teaspoons salt**
½ **cup bacon, cut fine**	½ **teaspoon dried thyme**
2 **large onions, sliced**	4 **bay leaves**
2 **large carrots, sliced**	1 **grated potato**
1 **cup chopped celery**	1 **ham hock**
2 **quarts water**	2 **tablespoons lemon juice**
½ **teaspoon white pepper**	**Sliced lemon**

Wash lentils. Drain. Saute bacon and onion until onion is golden. Add all ingredients except lemon. Cover and simmer for 3 hours. Remove ham hock and bay leaves. Cut up meat from ham hock and return to soup. Add lemon juice. Serve hot with lemon slices on top. Makes 10 to 12 servings.

HAM CHOWDER SOUP

2 **medium potatoes**	**Dash pepper**
1 **cup chopped onion**	3 **cups milk**
3 **tablespoons butter or**	1½ **cups chopped cooked ham**
margarine	1½ **cups shredded process**
3 **tablespoons flour**	**American cheese**

Peel potatoes and cook in boiling water. Cube when cooled. Reserve liquid. Add enough water to make 1 cup in pan. Cook onion in butter until tender, not brown. Blend in flour and pepper. Add milk and potato water together. Cook and stir until mixture thickens. Add ham, potatoes and cheese. Stir until cheese melts. Makes 4 to 5 servings.

HEARTY TURKEY SOUP

Garlic bread or crackers and a tossed salad make it a meal.

¼ cup butter or margarine	1 cup diced cooked turkey
2 tablespoons chopped onion	1 cup frozen
1 teaspoon curry powder	French green beans
1 cup diced potatoes	1 teaspoon minced, fresh
½ cup diced carrots	oregano, or ½ teaspoon dried
½ cup diagonally sliced celery	1 tablespoon minced parsley
3 cups turkey broth (or chicken)	1 14½-ounce can evaporated milk or 1⅔ cups light cream
1 teaspoon salt	2 tablespoons flour
¼ teaspoon pepper	

Melt butter in large Dutch oven and cook onion until transparent. Stir in curry powder and cook a minute or two longer. Stir in potatoes, carrots, celery, broth, salt and pepper and bring to a boil. Transfer to 300° oven and bake 10 to 15 minutes (or cook entirely on range on low heat). Stir in green beans, turkey, oregano and parsley and continue baking about 15 minutes or until vegetables are barely tender, but still a little crisp. Blend milk into flour, add to mixture, cook and stir until bubbly. Soup will be slightly thickened. Makes 4 to 6 servings.

SEAFOOD BISQUE

Serve with crisp spinach salad and crusty bread for an easy company luncheon.

1 10½-ounce can condensed cream of celery soup	1 7½-ounce can crab meat, drained and flaked
1 10¾-ounce can condensed cream of mushroom soup	1 4½-ounce can shrimp, drained
3 cups milk	1 teaspoon onion salt
	¼ teaspoon seasoned pepper
	1 cup sliced fresh mushrooms

Combine all ingredients; simmer, covered, 30 minutes. Stir occasionally. Makes 6 servings.

FRENCH CHICKEN ONION SOUP

A delicious, lighter version of the traditional French onion soup, using chicken broth instead of beef.

2 medium onions, thinly sliced
2 tablespoons butter or margarine
2 13¾-ounce cans chicken broth
¼ cup dry sherry
1 cup shredded Cheddar cheese
4 slices toasted French bread, about ½-inch thick

Cook onion slices in butter until soft. Add chicken broth and simmer until onion is tender, about 5 minutes. Add sherry. Place toast on bottom of individual casseroles or 2-quart casserole. Top with cheese. Pour soup over. Bake in 350° oven 10 minutes. Makes 4 servings.

MINESTRONE

1 cup chopped onions
½ cup olive oil
3 tablespoons butter or margarine
2 large potatoes diced
2 medium zucchini diced
1 cup diced carrots
1 cup diced celery
1 cup diced green beans
1 15-ounce can Italian tomatoes
1 15-ounce can kidney beans
6 cups beef broth
1-inch square piece of Parmesan cheese
Grated Parmesan for table service

Saute onions in oil and butter in large kettle. When wilted, add remaining ingredients, except Parmesan cheese. Cover when it comes to a boil and simmer gently 1 hour. Add the piece of cheese and continue simmering for an additional 20 to 30 minutes. May be frozen or refrigerated for days. Reheat and serve with plenty of grated Parmesan cheese. Makes 8 servings.

Pasta Fagioli: Process leftover minestrone in processor or blender. Remove to saucepan. Add uncooked pasta of your choice, cook over medium-low heat 1 hour. Serve in shallow bowls with crusty bread.

THE VICE PRESIDENT'S HOUSE
WASHINGTON, D.C. 20501

ALL AMERICAN CLAM CHOWDER

3 slices bacon
1/2 cup minced onions
1 - 7 1/2 oz. can minced clams
    (save clam liquor)
1 cup cubed potatoes
1 can cream of celery soup
1 1/2 cups milk
Dash of pepper

Cook bacon in frying pan until crisp. Remove
and break into one inch pieces. Brown onion
in bacon fat. Add clam liquor and potatoes.
Cover and cook over low heat until potatoes
are done (about 15 minutes). Blend in bacon
pieces, minced clams, and other ingredients.
Heat, but do <u>not</u> boil. Bacon may be used
for garnish.

Barbara Bush

CREAM OF CARROT SOUP SUPREME

2 tablespoons butter or margarine
1/3 cup chopped onion
2 tablespoons uncooked regular rice
1 cup sliced frozen carrots (or fresh)
1 13¾ can chicken broth (1¾ cups)
2 parsley sprigs
¼ teaspoon grated orange peel
¼ teaspoon sugar
Dash pepper
Dash celery salt
2 tablespoons orange juice
½ cup light cream

Melt butter or margarine. Add onion and rice and saute until onion is tender. Add carrots, chicken broth, parsley, orange peel, sugar and celery salt. Cover and cook slowly until vegetables are very tender, 20 minutes. Remove parsley sprigs. Pour soup into blender; cover and blend at high speed until smooth. Return soup to saucepan. Add orange juice, then cream. Heat just to boiling. Serve topped with snipped fresh parsley. Makes 6 small first-course servings.

SPRING SANDWICH PUFF

6 bread slices	¼ cup mayonnaise or salad
6 slices Cheddar or process	dressing
American cheese	¼ teaspoon salt
1 pound hot, cooked	Dash pepper
asparagus	3 egg whites
3 egg yolks	

In broiler toast bread on one side. Place cheese on untoasted side; broil to partially melt cheese. Remove from heat and place 3 or 4 spears of asparagus on top of each cheese slice.

Beat egg yolks until thick and lemon colored. Stir in mayonnaise, salt and pepper. Beat egg whites until stiff peaks are formed. Fold into egg yolk mixture. Pile mixture on top of asparagus. Bake in 350° oven about 13 minutes or until egg mixture is set. Makes 6 servings.

CRAB MEAT SANDWICHES

1 6 ounce can crab meat	Mayonnaise
1 8-ounce package cream cheese	8 tomato slices
1 tablespoon chopped onion	8 slices cheese, American
2 teaspoons Worcestershire	or Cheddar
sauce	8 Holland rusks

Mix all ingredients together, using just enough mayonnaise to moisten. Divide the mixture among the rusks. Place a slice of tomato and a slice of cheese on top. Heat in 325° oven for about 30 minutes or until heated through and cheese is melted. Makes 8 servings.

HOT TUNA SANDWICH

8 hot dog buns	2 tablespoons chopped green
¼ cup diced American cheese	pepper
3 hard cooked eggs	3 tablespoons chopped sweet
1 7-oz. can tuna	pickle
2 tablespoons chopped onion	½ cup mayonnaise

Split hot dog bun, dig out center. Fill with combined remaining ingredients; wrap with foil. Prick foil with fork. Heat in 350° oven for 30 minutes. Makes 8 servings.

SIDEWALK SANDWICHES

½ cup coarsely chopped
  tomatoes
¼ cup sliced onions
10 Greek olives, sliced (may
  substitute ripe olives)
1 tablespoon lemon juice

2 tablespoons olive oil
3 loaves pita bread
2 3-ounce packages cream
  cheese, softened
12 ounces meat (thin-sliced
  beef, corned beef, chicken,
  tuna)

Mix together tomatoes, onions, olives, lemon juice and olive oil. Cut each pita loaf in half, making two pockets. Spread one inside surface of each pocket with cream cheese. Stuff meat in, then fill with vegetable mixture. Makes 6 servings.

Variations: Spread bread with mayonnaise instead of cream cheese. Use grated cheese as another stuffing.

PITA TOASTS

A crisp accompaniment for soups, salads or casseroles —or use as an appetizer.

¾ cup butter or margarine,
  softened
2 tablespoons minced parsley
1 tablespoon snipped chives
1 tablespoon lemon juice

1 garlic clove, crushed
¼ teaspoon salt
Dash pepper
6 pita loaves

Cream butter. Beat in parsley, chives, lemon juice, garlic salt and pepper. Let stand at room temperature, covered, for at least 1 hour.

Halve pita loaves horizontally. Cut each half into 2 pieces and spread the inside of each piece with butter mixture. Arrange on baking sheet in one layer. Bake in 450° oven 5 minutes or until lightly browned and crisp.

Note: Twelve hard rolls, halved, may be substituted for pita loaves.

SANDWICH LOAF

1 1½-pound loaf unsliced Avocado Spread
   white bread, crust removed Vegetable Spread
Soft butter or margarine 2 8-ounce packages cream
Curried Egg Spread cheese, softened
Salmon Spread 2 tablespoons milk

Cut bread lengthwise 4 times to make 5 slices. Butter bread. Spread 1 slice with Curried Egg Spread, top with second slice. Repeat with Salmon Spread, Avocado Spread and Vegetable Spread.

Blend together cream cheese with milk. Spread over top and sides of sandwich loaf. Chill at least 4 hours. Before serving decorate with olives, pimiento and greens to make flowers.

Curried Egg Spread: Stir together 4 hard-cooked eggs, chopped, 2 teaspoons curry powder and ¼ cup mayonnaise.

Salmon Spread: Stir together 1 7-ounce can salmon, drained and flaked, ¼ cup chopped celery, ¼ cup chopped ripe olives, 2 tablespoons chili sauce, 1 tablespoon mayonnaise and 1 tablespoon lemon juice.

Avocado Spread: Mash 2 ripe avocados. Combine with 6 slices bacon crisp-cooked and crumbled, 2 tablespoons sliced green onion, 3 tablespoons lemon juice, 3 tablespoons mayonnaise, ¼ teaspoon salt and a dash of pepper.

Vegetable Spread: Combine 1 cup chopped celery, 1 cup chopped cucumber, ½ cup chopped Bermuda onion, ¼ cup chopped green pepper, 6 ripe olives, chopped, and ½ cup mayonnaise.

MOSTACCIOLI SALAD DELUXE

1 16-oz. package mostaccioli, 1 medium onion, finely
   cooked and drained chopped
1 medium cucumber, pared, 1 2-oz. jar chopped pimiento,
   seeded and diced drained
1 tablespoon flaked parsley Flavorful Sweet-Sour Dressing

In large bowl, combine drained mostaccioli, cucumber, onion, pimiento, and parsley; stir gently. Stir in Dressing. Cover and chill. Stir occasionally. Refrigerate 24 hours before serving. Keeps well. Makes 8 to 10 servings.

Flavorful Sweet-Sour Dressing: Combine 1½ cups sugar and 1½ cups cider vinegar. Bring to boiling, stirring to dissolve sugar. Whisk in ¼ cup salad oil, 2 tablespoons prepared mustard, 1 teaspoon salt, 1 teaspoon garlic powder and ½ teaspoon pepper. Cool.

BURGUNDY SALAD

1 6-ounce package raspberry-flavored gelatin
2 cups boiling water
½ cup Burgundy

1 16-ounce can cranberry sauce (with whole berries)
1 cup crushed pineapple
⅓ cup chopped nuts

Dissolve gelatin in boiling water. Add wine. Refrigerate until partially set. Add remaining ingredients. Pour into mold or 13x9x2-inch pan. When firm, top with Cheese Fluff Dressing. Makes 12 servings.

Cheese Fluff Dressing: Whip 1 2-ounce package whipped topping mix according to directions on package. Slowly add 1 8-ounce package cream cheese, softened, a little at a time. Add 1 tablespoon grated orange peel and 1 teaspoon vanilla. Beat well.

MELON DE MENTHE

Marinate slices of cantaloupe or honeydew melon in white creme de menthe for several hours, basting occasionally. Makes a refreshing, minty companion for chicken or seafood salad. Melon balls may also be used and combined with other fruit before serving.

CANTALOUPE BUFFET SALAD

3 cups thin sliced fresh cantaloupe
1 cucumber, peeled and thinly sliced

Black Pepper Dressing
Crisp Lettuce
Finely-snipped parsley

Gently toss cucumbers and melon with Black Pepper Dressing. Cover and chill 2 hours or longer.

To serve, arrange on lettuce-lined chilled serving platter or individual plates. Spoon dressing over and sprinkle with chopped parsley. Makes 4 servings.

Black Pepper Dressing: Shake together ½ cup salad oil, 3 tablespoons fresh lemon juice, ¾ teaspoon Dijon-style mustard, ½ teaspoon salt, and ½ teaspoon freshly ground black pepper.

In 1895, Hubbell gave a party at Terrace Hill to celebrate the fortieth anniversary of his arrival in Fort Des Moines. He shared the occasion with other pioneers, including P.M. Casady, Hoyt Sherman, J. S. Polk, James Savery and Edwin Clapp. His diary for that day said, "Dinner at 7. Dispersed at 10 p.m. Good time, they said. Wanted me to send for them at the end of another forty years."

MOLDED TOMATO SOUP SALAD

2 envelopes unflavored
gelatin
½ cup cold water
1 10¾-ounce can condensed
tomato soup
2 3-ounce packages cream
cheese

1 tablespoon lemon juice
1 cup mayonnaise or salad
dressing
½ cup chopped green pepper
½ cup chopped celery
¼ cup minced onion
¼ cup sliced green olives

Soften gelatin in cold water. Heat soup in saucepan over low heat. Add gelatin, stirring until dissolved. Remove from heat. Add cream cheese, beating with rotary beater until smooth. Cool. Fold in lemon juice, mayonnaise and vegetables.

Oil a 1½-quart mold or individual molds. Pour in salad mixture. Chill until set. Makes 10 servings.

CRAB LOUIS

3 cups mayonnaise or salad
dressing
½ cup chili sauce
¼ cup sweet pickle relish
½ cup chopped green pepper
1 rib celery, chopped
2 tablespoons finely chopped
onion

1 hard-cooked egg, chopped
1½ tablespoons lemon juice
6 cups shredded lettuce
1 6-ounce package frozen crab
meat, thawed, or 1 6-
ounce can crab meat, drained
and flaked

Combine salad dressing, chili sauce, pickle relish, green pepper, celery, onion, egg and lemon juice. Chill.

Place lettuce in salad bowl. Top with crab meat, then dressing. Makes 6 servings.

ANTIPASTO SALAD

Main course for lunch, or first course for your Italian dinner.

1 cup rice	1 2-ounce can anchovies, drained
1 cup sliced celery	and chopped, optional
1 6-ounce jar marinated	¼ cup olive oil
artichoke hearts, drained	1 tablespoon lemon juice
1 cup sliced mushrooms	1 teaspoon salt
1 9 ¼-ounce can tuna,	½ teaspoon freshly ground black
drained and flaked	pepper
1 cup peeled diced tomatoes	½ teaspoon capers
½ cup sliced ripe olives	1 red onion, sliced thin and
	separated into rings

Cook rice as directed on package. Drain, cool and toss with a fork to keep grains separate. Add celery, artichokes, mushrooms, tuna, tomatoes, olives and anchovies. Toss together with 2 forks.

Combine oil, lemon juice, salt, pepper and capers. Pour over salad and toss. Heap on a serving dish and arrange onion slices on top. Makes 6 servings.

CHICKEN-ARTICHOKE SALAD

Interesting flavors in a piquant luncheon salad.

1 8-ounce package chicken-	2 6-ounce jars marinated
flavored rice-vermicelli	artichoke hearts, drained
mixture	(juice reserved)
6 green onions, sliced	⅓ cup mayonnaise
¼ cup sliced stuffed green	¼ teaspoon curry powder
olives	2 cups diced cooked chicken
½ cup chopped green pepper	

Prepare rice-vermicelli mixture as on package, omitting butter. Combine with onions, olives and green pepper. Mix with marinade, mayonnaise and curry. Slice artichoke hearts and add with chicken. Toss lightly. Makes 8 servings.

CURRIED CHICKEN WITH FRESH FRUIT SALAD

A fine choice for curry lovers. Rich-tasting elegance for a special luncheon.

3   cups cubed cooked chicken
¼   cup bottled oil and
    vinegar dressing
½   cup mayonnaise or salad
    dressing
1   tablespoon chopped
    preserved ginger
2   teaspoons curry powder
1   teaspoon grated onion

½   teaspoon salt
½   cup heavy cream, whipped
2   cups fresh pineapple chunks,
    or 1 20-ounce can pineapple
    chunks, drained
1   large apple, unpeeled and diced
1½ cups seedless grapes
¼   cup chutney
¼   cup green pepper, chopped
    Crisp lettuce

Marinate chicken in salad dressing 2 hours; drain. Meanwhile, combine mayonnaise, ginger, curry powder, onion and salt. Fold in whipped cream.

Combine chicken, fruit, green pepper and curried mayonnaise. Serve in lettuce cups garnished with red cherries. Makes 6 to 8 servings.

PARTY CHICKEN SALAD

Men enjoy this crunchy salad.

4   cups cubed cooked chicken
1   cup grated carrots
1   cup finely chopped
    celery
1   cup sliced ripe olives
1   cup green seedless grapes or
    1 cup mandarin oranges

1   tablespoon grated onion
1   cup mayonnaise or salad
    dressing
1½ cups frozen whipped dessert
    topping, thawed, or ¾ cups
    heavy cream, whipped
2   cups canned shoestring potatoes

Combine all ingredients except shoestring potatoes. Chill 3 to 5 hours. Add potatoes just before serving. Serve in lettuce cups. Makes 8 servings.

ROAST BEEF SALAD PROVENCALE

A glass of red wine and a checkered tablecloth, and you'll think you're in the south of France!

1 pound green beans, cooked and drained (or use canned)
Mustard French Dressing (below)
2 pounds potatoes, boiled, peeled and thinly sliced
¼ cup minced shallots
3 tablespoons hot beef broth

2 red onions, thinly sliced and separated into rings
2 pounds cooked roast beef (¼-inch slices cut in 2-inch squares)
Chopped chives
Chopped parsley

Toss green beans with ½ cup dressing. Set aside. Combine potatoes with shallots. Sprinkle with broth and toss until broth is absorbed. Add ½ cup dressing and toss potatoes to coat them.

Arrange rings of onions, green beans, potatoes and roast beef in layers in bowl. Sprinkle with chives and parsley. Serve at room temperature. Serves 6.

Mustard French Dressing: In a bowl beat together thoroughly with fork or whisk ¼ cup white wine vinegar, 2 tablespoons Dijon-style mustard, 1 teaspoon salt and pepper to taste. Gradually beat in 1 cup imported olive oil. Mix well.

HOT CHICKEN DELIGHT

4 cups cooked, cooled chicken chunks
4 hard cooked eggs, sliced
2 cups chopped celery
2 pimientos, snipped
1 teaspoon minced onion
¾ cup mayonnaise
¾ cup cream of chicken soup

2 tablespoons lemon juice
1 teaspoon salt
½ teaspoon monosodium glutamate
1½ cups crushed potato chips
1 cup grated cheese
⅔ cup chopped toasted almonds

Combine all but last three ingredients. Place in large rectangular dish and top with chips, cheese and almonds. Let stand in refrigerator overnight, then bake at 400° for 20 to 25 minutes. Serves 8.

CHICKEN IN FILO

A special treatment of chicken for a special luncheon.

10 to 12 sheets filo dough
1 cup chopped celery
2/3 cup chopped onion
1 tablespoon butter or margarine
2 cups chopped, cooked chicken

2 tablespoons chicken broth
2 teaspoons dried parsley flakes
1/2 teaspoon salt
1/8 teaspoon pepper
1 beaten egg
6 tablespoons butter or margarine, melted
Greek Lemon Egg Sauce

Thaw filo dough at room temperature 2 hours. Cook onion and celery in 1 tablespoon butter in covered skillet until tender. Stir occasionally. Add chicken and chicken broth. Cook, stirring constantly, uncovered, until all the broth is absorbed. Stir in parsley, salt and pepper. Remove from heat. Stir in egg.

For each roll, stack half the sheets of filo dough, brushing some of the 6 tablespoons melted butter between each layer. Spoon 1¼ cups chicken mixture over filo leaves to within 1 inch of edges. Turn one short side over filling about 1 inch; fold in long sides. Roll as for jelly roll, starting at folded short side. Place, seam side down, on a lightly greased shallow baking pan. Repeat with remaining filo and filling. Score each roll into 3 or 4 portions. Bake in 350° oven 40 minutes, or until rolls are browned. Cut rolls where scored. Serve with Greek Lemon Sauce along with hot cooked rice. Makes 6 to 8 servings.

Greek Lemon Egg Sauce: Melt 2 tablespoons butter or margarine in saucepan; stir in 2 tablespoons flour and 1/8 teaspoon salt. Add 1¼ cups chicken broth all at once. Cook and stir until mixture is thick and bubbly. Stir together 2 beaten egg yolks and 4 teaspoons lemon juice. Stir about half of hot mixture into egg yolk mixture. Return to remaining hot mixture in saucepan. Cook and stir 2 minutes more. If made ahead, reheat to serve.

In 1897 the Hubbells opened Terrace Hill to 500 guests gathered in Des Moines for a women's suffrage convention. Some of the leading suffragettes in America were in attendance. A description of the party said that guests were led to the dining room, where coffee and confections were served from a table beautifully decorated in yellow and blue. The centerpiece consisted of an immense jardiniere of yellow jonquils resting on yellow embroidered linen and set off by burning white tapers in tall candelabra.

LOBSTER STRUDEL

An elegant entree suitable for a special lunch, dinner or late supper.

1 8-ounce package cream cheese	1 tablespoon chopped dill
1 cup sour cream	or ½ teaspoon dried dill
1 teaspoon salt	1 pound mushrooms
1 egg	3 tablespoons butter or
4 8-ounce lobster tails, cooked	margarine
1 tablespoon chopped chives	8 filo leaves
	Melted butter

Cream the cheese and beat in 1 cup sour cream. Add salt and egg. Cut lobster meat into large pieces and blend with cheese mixture. Add chives and dill. Slice mushrooms and saute them in 3 tablespoons butter. Season. Strain and press well and add to above mixture. Butter well a 12 x 7½ x 2-inch baking dish. Place 4 layers of filo leaves on bottom, buttering well between each layer. Pour in filling. Place 4 more leaves on top, buttering as before. Fold in and roll up sides all around. Brush with butter and bake at 375° for 35 minutes. Makes 6 servings.

Crab Meat Casserole

1 No. 2 can artichoke hearts	1 t. Worchestershire sauce
1 lb. crab meat	¼ cup med. dry sherry
½ lb. fresh mushrooms	Paprika to taste
4 T. butter	Cayenne to taste
2½ T. flour	Pepper to taste
1 cup cream	¼ cup Parmesan cheese, grated
½ t. salt	

Place artichokes in bottom of baking dish; spread a layer of crab meat. Add a layer of sauted mushrooms. Melt butter in a saucepan; add remaining ingredients except cheese, stirring well after each addition to form a smooth sauce. Pour sauce over artichoke-crab layers and sprinkle cheese on top. Bake 20 minutes at 375 degrees.

Yield: 8 servings.

With best wishes, Nancy Reagan

HAM STROGANOFF

Quick, easy and delicious favorite for brunch, lunch or supper.

1	10-ounce package frozen puff pastry shells, baked	1	10¾-ounce can condensed cream of chicken soup
3	cups cooked ham, diced	1	cup sour cream
½	cup chopped onion	⅓	cup milk
2	tablespoons butter or margarine	½	teaspoon paprika
½	cup sliced ripe olives	⅓	cup toasted slivered almonds

Saute ham and onion in butter until the onion is tender but not brown. Stir in the olives. Combine the soup, sour cream, milk and paprika until smooth and add the ham mixture. Cook and stir over medium heat until heated through. Do not boil. Spoon into pastry shells. Sprinkle with almonds. Makes 6 servings.

SHRIMP JAMBALAYA

3	slices bacon, diced	1	teaspoon salt
3	tablespoons chopped onion		Dash cayenne
3	tablespoons chopped celery	½	teaspoon MSG
3	tablespoons chopped parsley	3	cups cooked rice
3	tablespoons chopped green pepper	1	cup cooked shrimp, broken in pieces
1	tablespoon flour	1	cup diced ham
4	cups tomatoes, cooked or canned	1	cup cooked chicken

Fry bacon. Add onion, celery, parsley and green pepper. Cook and stir until onion is yellow. Add flour and stir until slightly brown. Add tomatoes, salt, cayenne and MSG. Cook slowly until thick. Add rice, shrimp, chicken and ham and stir well. Makes 8 servings.

CHICKEN LOAF

3	cups diced chicken	2	cups toasted bread crumbs
4	eggs slightly beaten	1	teaspoon salt
3	tablespoons chopped celery	1/8	teaspoon pepper
3	cups chicken broth		

Mix ingredients; put in loaf pan. Bake at 350° 1 hour.

APPETIZERS
AND
BEVERAGES

SESAME CRAB ROLLS

A hit at any party.

½ pound processed American cheese, cubed	20 slices bread
½ cup butter	1 cup butter
2 6-ounce cans crabmeat, drained	1½ 1 7/8-ounce cans sesame seeds

Melt cheese and ½ cup butter in double boiler. Cool slightly and add crabmeat. Stir until cool. (Mixture will blend as it cools.)

Cut crusts from bread and flatten slices with rolling pin. Spread mixture on one side and roll up in jelly roll fashion. Melt remaining cup butter. Dip each roll in melted butter and roll in sesame seeds. Place on cookie sheet and freeze. Thaw about 15 minutes. Cut rolls in thirds and broil, turning once. Makes 60 rolls.

HOT RYE ROUNDS

These can go from freezer to broiler any time there is a party.

1 pound ground beef	½ teaspoon dried oregano
1 pound hot pork sausage	½ teaspoon garlic powder
1 pound process cheese food	2 loaves party rye bread

Brown together and stir ground beef and pork sausage. Drain off all drippings. Stir in cheese and melt. Add oregano and garlic powder. Spread on individual party rye rounds while warm. Put on cookie sheets, freeze, then bag.

To serve, heat under broiler until bubbly. Makes 48.

TOASTY CRAB BITES

1 8-oz. package cream cheese, softened	1 teaspoon horseradish
1 7½-oz. can crab meat, drained	1 teaspoon Worcestershire sauce
1 tablespoon mayonnaise	Salt and pepper to taste
1 tablespoon finely chopped onion	36 1½-inch bread rounds, slightly toasted

Mix first seven ingredients and spread on bread rounds. Bake 350° for 10 to 15 minutes. Makes 32.

ARTICHOKE HEART SNACKS

These can be made in advance and frozen. Thaw slightly before baking.

1   loaf thin-sliced bread, cut
    in rounds or squares (no
    crusts)
1   cup mayonnaise

1   cup grated Parmesan cheese
1   6-ounce jar marinated
    artichoke hearts, drained and
    quartered

Combine mayonnaise and cheese. Frost each bread round with mixture. Top with a piece of artichoke heart. Bake in 375° oven for 10 to 12 minutes. Serve hot.

STUFFED EGGS WITH CAVIAR

These magnificent eggs are fit for a palace. Use them to garnish a cold main dish platter or as part of an elegant relish tray.

Cut hard-cooked eggs in half. Mash yolks and blend with plain mayonnaise. Fill egg-white halves evenly. Cover yolk mixture with black caviar. Coat the cooked white edge with mayonnaise and sprinkle with minced parsley and finely minced onion. Spoon Gelee (p. 22) over caviar.

The marriage of the Hubbells' daughter Beulah, just before the turn of the century, rivaled the Allens' 1869 housewarming for opulence. Miss Hubbell married Swedish count Carl Wachtmeister, whom she had met in Chicago at the Swedish consulate. Among the 700 guests were nobility from several European nations, members of the Des Moines aristocracy, and guests from Chicago and Washington, D.C.

The bridal party assembled on the landing of the great staircase and the vows were said under the great parlor chandelier. The bride wore a white satin brocade court gown, which she had worn when presented to royalty at the court of St. James.

CHILI PEPPERS AND CHEESE

1   4-ounce can green chili   3   eggs
peppers, drained and seeded   2   tablespoons water
14   ounces grated Cheddar
cheese

Place chilis and cheese in 9-inch pie plate. Blend together eggs and water. Pour over cheese. Refrigerate at least one hour. Bake in 350° oven 35 to 40 minutes or until slightly brown. Let cool and cut into bite-size pieces.

CHEDDAR BISCUITS

A nippy appetizer that will keep longer than you'll have any left to keep.

½   cup butter   ½   teaspoon salt
½   pound sharp Cheddar   1   dash tabasco sauce
cheese, grated   Walnut halves
1½   cups all-purpose flour

Cream butter and cheese together until smooth; cut in flour, salt and tabasco sauce and blend well. Form into balls about the size of golf balls. Cover and chill at least 4 hours, or overnight. Slice balls into ½-inch slices. Sprinkle ungreased baking sheet lightly with salt and place slices on sheet. Press walnut half into each biscuit. Bake in 350° oven 7 to 8 minutes, or until golden. Serve warm or at room temperature. Store tightly covered. Makes 6 dozen.

PARMESAN GLAZED WALNUTS

1½   cups walnut halves   ¼   teaspoon salt
1   tablespoon butter, melted   ¼   cup shredded Parmesan
¼   teaspoon hickory smoked   cheese
salt

Heat oven to 350°. Spread walnuts in shallow pan and toast in oven for 10 minutes. Mix butter, hickory salt and salt and toss lightly with walnuts. Sprinkle cheese over top and stir. Return to oven and toast 3 to 4 minutes. Makes 1½ cups.

HAWAIIAN MEATBALLS

1½ pounds ground beef	¾ cup milk
2 eggs	1 teaspoon salt
2 tablespoons minced onion	¼ teaspoon pepper
¾ cup soft bread crumbs	Butter or margarine

Combine ingredients. Form 1-inch balls, brown in butter or margarine and drain. Place in sauce and serve warm with toothpicks.

Sauce: In saucepan over medium heat, cook 3 cups pineapple juice, ½ cup dark brown sugar, 6 crushed ginger snaps, 2 tablespoons butter and a pinch of salt. Cook until thickened.

SESAME WINGS

Have plenty of napkins and a bone plate available for these guest-pleasing hors d'oeuvres.

1 24-ounce bottle soy sauce	2 cups sauterne wine
1 teaspoon ground ginger	1 clove crushed garlic
1 cup brown sugar, packed	4 dozen chicken wings, cut in half

Combine and boil for ½ hour the first five ingredients. Cook the wings for 15 minutes in the soy sauce mixture. Remove and drain on cooling racks with paper towels underneath. Sprinkle with sesame seeds. This much can be done ahead; freeze if desired.

Before serving, place in 400° oven for about 15 minutes or until warm.

HOT SAUSAGE PUFFS

3 cups biscuit mix	10 ounces sharp process American cheese, softened
1 pound hot sausage, cooked and crumbled	Water

Mix together all ingredients, adding enough water to hold ingredients together. Form into balls and place on cookie sheet. Bake in 400° oven for 10 to 12 minutes. May be frozen if desired. Add a few more minutes to baking time if frozen. Makes 6 to 8 dozen.

ONION AND GREEN PEPPER SANDWICHES

Garden-fresh taste in these tea table perfect sandwiches.

3 green peppers, seeded and chopped	1 8-ounce package cream cheese
1 large Bermuda onion,	1 pint mayonnaise
1 tablespoon sugar	1 loaf bread
1 teaspoon salt	Butter or margarine

In food processor or blender, grind the pepper and onion together thoroughly. Place in bowl and add sugar and salt. Cover with water and let stand overnight. When ready to use, drain off all liquid and wring out mixture in cloth.

Beat the cream cheese and mayonnaise together with electric mixer and add the pepper and onion mixture.

Trim crusts from bread and butter each piece. Spread pepper-onion mixture on half of slices. Top with remaining buttered slices. Cut in fingers or any desired shape. Wrap tightly and refrigerate until ready to serve.

CURRIED CHUTNEY MOLD

A wonderful combination of taste and textures. Don't count on any leftovers!

11 oz. of cream cheese	½ lb. bacon, cooked crisp and crumbled
1 3-oz. package raisins, chopped	½ cup chopped green onion
3 tablespoons sour cream	1 8½-oz. jar chutney
3 teaspoons curry powder	Flaked coconut
½ (6½-oz.) can cocktail peanuts, chopped coarsely	1 small pineapple, optional

By hand, mix first seven ingredients (do not use a mixer). Add ½ of the chutney (snip any large pieces); reserve remaining chutney.

If desired, halve pineapple; remove fruit, leaving at least ½-inch shell. (Use pineapple for garnish or for another purpose.) Spoon cheese mixture in pineapple halves or bowl. Top with remaining chutney; sprinkle with flaked coconut. Serve with rye rounds, melba toast rounds, or wheat thins.

MOUSSE DE JAMBON (Ham Mousse)

A subtle blend of flavors that will appeal to the gourmet. If mousse is to be coated and decorated, do this the day before. Decorations will keep and flavors in the mousse will have a chance to develop.

Recipe of Gelee	¼ cup Madeira
1 tablespoon gelatin	1 tablespoon Cognac
¼ cup cold water	1 cup heavy cream,
½ recipe of Chaud-Froid	whipped
2 tablespoons horseradish	3 tablespoons confectioners'
½ teaspoon salt	sugar
3 cups diced ham	2 tablespoons Grand Marnier

Make Gelee (p. 22) and have ready to use. Soak gelatin in cold water. Make ½ recipe of Chaud-Froid (P. 23) Add soaked gelatin to hot Chaud-Froid and stir until dissolved. Put the Chaud-Froid, horseradish, salt, ham, Madeira and Cognac into blender or food processor. Whirl to blend. Refrigerate ham mixture until cold, but do not allow to set.

Whip cream to very stiff. Add sugar, then fold into the ham mixture. Add Grand Marnier. Mix well and pack into 4-cup mold. Refrigerate until set.

When ready to decorate, unmold and place on cardboard or paper plate cut to fit.

If you do not wish to decorate: Before putting ham mixture in mold, pour a ¼-inch layer of Gelee into bottom of mold. Sprinkle with 2 tablespoons minced parsley. Refrigerate until set. Pack mold with ham mixture and coat with Gelee. Cover and refrigerate 8 hours or overnight.

Photographs taken the day of the wedding of Beulah Hubbell showed how parts of the mansion looked at the turn of the century. In the dining room was a door opening into a large butler's pantry equipped with a sink, icebox, warming stove, serving counter, and dumbwaiter used to carry prepared food from the ground floor kitchen to the first floor dining room, which contained a massive built-in buffet and ornate shelving over the marble fireplace.

SALMON BALL

1 1-pound can salmon	1 teaspoon prepared
1 8-ounce package cream	horseradish
cheese, softened	¼ teaspoon salt
1 tablespoon lemon juice	¼ teaspoon liquid smoke
2 teaspoons grated onion	½ cup chopped pecans
	3 tablespoons snipped parsley

Combine first seven ingredients. Chill. Shape into ball and roll in pecans and parsley. Serve with crackers.

SMOKED SALMON AND PUMPERNICKEL

1 pound round loaf	½ cup sour cream
pumpernickel, unsliced	⅓ cup chopped scallions
½ pound smoked salmon	1 tablespoon lemon juice
1 8-ounce package cream	Capers, drained
cheese	

Cut 1 inch off top of loaf; cut a 3 to 4 inch circle out of the center. Tear the removed bread into bite size pieces for dipping. Combine the remaining ingredients except the capers and mix well. Carefully fold in the capers and chill. Just before serving, fill the bread cavity with the mixture. Place on a platter and surround with the bread pieces and serve. Guests dip the bread pieces into the salmon mixture. When the bread pieces are gone, tear the sides of the loaf apart and eat.

AVOCADO SHRIMP MOLD

2 large ripe avocados	¼ teaspoon each salt, white
¼ cup garlic olive oil	pepper and onion powder
¼ cup lemon or lime juice	¼ cup mayonnaise
1 envelope gelatin	2 6½-oz. cans shrimp, drained
3 tablespoons water	and chopped
	1 cup heavy cream, whipped

Peel and dice avocado, marinate in oil and lemon or lime juice 2 hours. Soften gelatin in cold water; dissolve over hot water. Cool. In blender, puree avocado and juices, gelatin, seasonings, mayonnaise and shrimp. Fold in cream. Pour into a 4 to 5 cup mold, cover and chill at least 6 hours. Turn mold out onto serving platter and garnish with parsley and lemon slices. Serve with melba rounds or other plain crackers. Makes about 40 servings.

SMOKED SALMON SPREAD

For a really special occasion, add 2 ounces of red caviar—fit for a czar!

4 ounces sliced smoked salmon	2 tablespoons diced onion
8 ounces cream cheese, softened	¼ cup heavy cream
¼ cup butter or margarine, softened	4 teaspoons lemon juice
	2 large sprigs parsley
	¼ teaspoon white pepper

Cut salmon into ½-inch squares. Put all ingredients into a blender or food processor. Blend until smooth. Chill. Serve with plain crackers or party rye bread.

CAVIAR SPREAD

This elegant hors d'oeuvre never fails to please both guest and hostess for its rich flavor and ease of preparation.

6 hard-cooked eggs, chopped	¼ cup mayonnaise
2 tablespoons butter or margarine, melted	1 cup sour cream
½ cup onion, chopped	1 4-ounce jar lumpfish caviar
	Lemon wedges (optional)

Combine eggs, butter or margarine and onion in glass pie plate or quiche dish. Cover and refrigerate overnight. Mix mayonnaise and sour cream and spread on top of egg mixture and spread caviar over top of this. Decorate with lemon wedges and serve with crackers or party rye.

TUNA CHEESE DIP

1 8-oz. package cream cheese	½ teaspoon salt
1 8-oz. carton sour cream	½ teaspoon pepper
1 16-oz. carton cottage cheese	¼ teaspoon monosodium glutamate
1 9-oz. can tuna, drained	
1 small onion, finely chopped	¼ cup chili sauce
½ teaspoon Worcestershire sauce	1 tablespoon lemon juice

Blend well. (Will be slightly lumpy.) Serve with raw vegetables, potato chips or fritos.

ARTICHOKE SPREAD

1 14-ounce can artichoke hearts, drained	¼ cup mayonnaise or salad dressing
1 8-ounce package cream cheese, softened	¼ cup sour cream
	¼ cup chopped green onion

Cut artichoke hearts into sections. Place in mixing bowl with all ingredients and mix with electric mixer. Refrigerate. Warm to room temperature to serve. Frost with caviar, if desired. Serve with a mild cracker.

CRAB MEAT REMOULADE

1 6-ounce can crab meat, drained	2 tablespoons lemon juice
1 cup mayonnaise or salad dressing	2 cloves garlic, crushed
¼ cup olive oil	1 teaspoon celery seed
	2 ribs celery, chopped
	¼ teaspoon salt
	1/8 teaspoon pepper

Pick over and shred crab meat. Blend all ingredients by hand. Refrigerate. Serve with crackers, chips and raw vegetables. Makes 2½ cups.

SHRIMP BUTTER

This is a winner that keeps well in the refrigerator.

1 4½-ounce can shrimp, drained	4 tablespoons mayonnaise
½ cup butter, softened	2 tablespoons lemon juice
8 ounces cream cheese, softened	1 tablespoon minced onion
	¼ teaspoon salt

Mix all ingredients and blend thoroughly with mixer, blender or food processor. Refrigerate to blend flavors. Serve with crackers or Melba toast. Store covered in refrigerator. Makes 2 cups.

"Plains Special" Cheese Ring

1 pound grated sharp cheese
1 cup finely chopped nuts
1 cup mayonnaise
1 small onion, finely grated

Black pepper
Dash cayenne
Strawberry preserves, optional

Combine all ingredients except preserves, season to taste with pepper. Mix well and place in a 5 or 6 cup lightly greased ring mold. Refrigerate until firm for several hours or overnight.

To serve, unmold, and if desired, fill center with strawberry preserves, or serve plain with crackers.

With best wishes, Rosalynn Carter

ALMOND-BACON-CHEDDAR SPREAD

⅓   cup toasted chopped
     almonds
6   slices bacon, crisp-cooked
     and crumbled
1½ cups grated sharp cheddar
     cheese
½   cup mayonnaise
1   tablespoon finely chopped
     onion
¼   teaspoon salt

Combine and mix lightly. (Can be made a day ahead.) Serve with crackers.

CHILI CHEESE LOG

1 8-ounce package cream
   cheese, softened
½ teaspoon Worcestershire
   sauce
1/8 teaspoon salt

Few drops tabasco sauce
1 or 2 cloves garlic, crushed
1 cup chopped pecans
2 to 4 tablespoons chili powder

Beat cream cheese until soft and smooth. Blend in remaining ingredients, except chili powder. Mix until smooth. (If very soft, refrigerate before handling.) Shape into a log about 1½ inches in diameter. Sprinkle chili powder on sheet of waxed paper. Roll log in chili powder to coat evenly. Wrap in waxed paper. Chill several hours until firm. Serve with unflavored round crackers.

SUMMER SAUSAGE APPETIZER

This unusual combination may be used as a spread or a dip.

1 8-ounce package cream cheese
1 3-ounce package cream cheese
⅓ 10¾-ounce can cream of
   mushroom soup
1 small clove garlic, crushed

1½ teaspoon lemon juice
Seasoned salt to taste
¼ teaspoon tabasco sauce
1 8-ounce package summer
   sausage, rind removed and
   diced

Blend all ingredients, except sausage, in electric mixer until smooth. Fold in sausage. Serve with crackers, party bread rounds or sturdy chips.

HERBED BUTTER CHIPS

Perfect at lunch as an accompaniment for soup or salad.

1 8-oz. package refrigerated
   butterflake dinner rolls

3 tablespoons melted butter or
   margarine
Fines herbes or salad seasoning

Separate the 12 rolls; split each into 4 or 5 rounds. Place in a single layer on greased large cookie sheet. Brush generously with melted butter or margarine. Sprinkle with fines herbes or salad seasoning. Bake at 400° 8 to 10 minutes or until crisp and lightly browned. Serve hot. Makes 4 to 5 dozen.

PARTY LIVER PATE

½ pound chicken or goose
   livers, quartered
1 small onion, halved
½ cup chicken stock or
   bouillon

½ teaspoon paprika
½ teaspoon curry powder
½ teaspoon salt
1 teaspoon Worcestershire sauce
1/8 teaspoon pepper
8 ounces cream cheese

Simmer liver and onion in broth for 8 minutes. Drain off any remaining liquid. Place all ingredients in blender or food processor. Blend until smooth; chill. Serve with crackers or toast rounds. Makes 3 cups.

TUNA MOUNTAIN

An attractive and delicious spread to serve with crackers or rye bread.

1 cup butter or margarine
1 8-ounce package cream cheese
2 7½-ounce cans tuna,
   drained
2 tablespoons chopped green
   onions
1 tablespoon lemon juice
1 tablespoon capers

¼ teaspoon salt
¼ teaspoon dried tarragon,
   crushed
Dash pepper
¼ cup finely snipped parsley
1 hard-cooked egg yolk, sieved
Radishes

Cream together butter and cream cheese. Beat in tuna, onions, lemon juice, capers, salt, tarragon, and pepper until smooth. Shape into a mountain on serving plate. Sprinkle parsley around base. Chill. Sprinkle top with sieved egg. Garnish mountain with whole radishes. Serve with crackers or rye bread. Makes 3½ cups spread.

FRESH SPINACH DIP

1 cup chopped fresh spinach	1 teaspoon salt
½ cup chopped parsley	1 teaspoon pepper
½ cup chopped green onions	2 cups mayonnaise

Wash spinach and squeeze dry. Combine all ingredients in blender or processor and blend until smooth. Serve with raw vegetables or thin wheat crackers. Makes 2 cups.

TEXAS TACO DIP

2 large tomatoes, chopped	1 teaspoon garlic salt
2 green peppers, chopped	3 tablespoons olive oil
3 green onions with tops, chopped	½ teaspoon salt
	¼ teaspoon pepper
1 4½-ounce can chopped ripe olives	2 tablespoons taco sauce

Mix all ingredients except taco sauce and chill several hours. Just before serving, add taco sauce. Serve with taco-flavored chips. Serves 6 to 8.

SPICY BEEF DIP

1 pound ground beef	¾ teaspoon dried oregano
1 cup chopped onion	1 teaspoon sugar
1 clove garlic, crushed	1 8-ounce package cream cheese
1 8-oz. can tomato sauce	
¼ cup catsup	⅓ cup grated Romano or Parmesan cheese

Brown beef, onion and garlic; spoon off fat. Add tomato sauce, catsup, oregano and sugar. Simmer 10 minutes. Mix in cheeses. Serve warm as dip with taco chips.

CHILI CON QUESO

2 tablespoons butter or
  margarine
1 small onion finely chopped
1 cup tomatoes, chopped
Salt and pepper

1 4-oz. can hot green chilies
½ pound shredded cheddar
  cheese (2 cups)
3 oz. cream cheese

Melt butter, stir in onion, tomatoes, salt, pepper and chilies. Simmer for 15 minutes. Add cheese. When cheese melts, stir in cream. Serve hot in chafing dish. Use as a dip for taco chips.

HOT CRAB DIP

This is always the first one gone at a cocktail party.

1 3-ounce package cream
  cheese
1 5-ounce jar sharp American
  process cheese spread
½ cup milk

1 7½-ounce can drained crab
  meat or 1 7½-ounce can
  drained minced clams
Dash Worcestershire sauce

Combine all ingredients in top of double boiler. Heat over boiling water, stirring occasionally, until cheese has melted and ingredients are well combined. Serve hot with chips or crackers.

In 1900, Hubbell prepared an inventory of every item in the house. He eventually included 592 items. For example: "Dining room—a Champlain marble fireplace with oak mantel glass, a brass fire set, and a red and gold Venetian glass punch bowl." In the inventory, many units were included as one item—for example, forty-eight blue-and-gold dinner plates with platters to match.

BAGNA CAUDA

The ancient custom of eating from the same dish to signify the spirit of good fellowship is beautifully presented in the spectacular Italian dish Bagna Cauda, or, as translated, "hot bath."

½ cup butter	1 2-ounce can flat anchovy
¼ cup olive oil	fillets, well drained, then
4 small cloves garlic, minced	finely chopped
or mashed	4 cups raw vegetables for
	dipping
	Thinly sliced French bread

Choose a heatproof container that will be only half filled by the sauce and add butter, oil, garlic and anchovies. Place over low heat until butter is melted; keep hot over a candle or alcohol flame and keep heat low enough to prevent browning or burning the sauce. Present sauce with a basket of the vegetables and another basket containing the bread.

Twirl a vegetable piece through the sauce. Hold a slice of bread under the vegetable to catch any drips as you prepare to eat it. Eventually, the bread soaks up enough sauce to become a delicious morsel, too. Makes 8 to 10 servings. Can be doubled or tripled.

Vegetable suggestions: artichoke leaves, cabbage chunks, cauliflower pieces, green beans, cherry tomatoes, green pepper chunks, mushrooms, turnips, radishes, zucchini.

The Hubbells used Terrace Hill for all manner of social functions. Every year Hubbell gave a dinner party to entertain members of the Des Moines City Council. Any differences of opinion were forgotten at the dinners, which were sometimes followed by poker games.

CHAMPAGNE PUNCH

For the ultimate celebration.

½ 5th of vodka

1 5th champagne, chilled
1 bottle ginger ale, chilled

Mix together, ice and serve. Makes 16 5-ounce servings.

SHERRY COOLER

1 bottle sherry
1 6-ounce can frozen lemonade
concentrate, thawed

2 tablespoons fresh lemon
juice
Dash bitters

Combine all ingredients; mix well. Chill several hours. Serve over ice. Makes 6 servings.

STRAWBERRY PUNCH

3 6-ounce cans frozen
lemonade concentrate

1 10-ounce package frozen
strawberries (or 1½ cups
fresh strawberries and ½ cup
sugar)
1 quart chilled ginger ale

Place strawberries, slightly thawed, in blender. Add lemonade and 3 cans of water. Cover and blend. Place in punch bowl or pitcher. Add gingerale. Makes 20 3-ounce servings.

WHITE WINE COOLER

Pretty in a punch bowl.

1 bottle chilled dry white wine	½ to 1 cup granulated sugar
1 bottle club soda	2 oranges

Just before serving, mix liquids in punch bowl and add sugar slowly to taste. Peel and dice one orange and add to mixture. Slice the other orange, unpeeled, into cubes and float on top of mixture. Ladle into wine glasses. Makes 12 5-ounce servings.

CATALAN SANGRIA

2 bottles red wine	1 orange, thinly sliced
1 bottle champagne	1 cinnamon stick

Fill a punch bowl with ice and pour the mixture over. Makes 10 to 12 servings.

WINE COOLER

1 bottle rose wine	1 16-ounce bottle 7-up (use diet beverage if preferred)

Pour equal amounts of rose and carbonated beverage into 4 tall glasses or tulip wine glasses. Fill with ice and serve.

GOLDEN SUNSHINE PITCHER PUNCH

1 6-ounce can frozen orange concentrate, thawed	3 cans cold water
	2 cups apricot nectar
1 6-ounce can frozen lemonade concentrate, thawed	1 quart lemon-lime-flavored carbonated beverage, chilled

In large pitcher combine orange juice concentrate, lemonade concentrate, water and apricot nectar. Stir well. Chill. Just before serving, add lemon-lime-carbonated beverage slowly to preserve bubbles. Serve in tall glasses over ice. Garnish with fresh mint. Makes 2½ quarts.

FROZEN DAIQUIRI

Refreshing warm weather drink.

1 **6-ounce can frozen limeade concentrate**	2 **cans water**
	1 **10-ounce bottle lemon-lime carbonated beverage**
2 **cans light rum**	

Combine all ingredients and place in a freezer container for several hours or overnight. Spoon into wine goblets and let set until slushy. Makes approximately 10 servings.

FROZEN STRAWBERRY DAIQUIRI

1 **10-ounce package frozen strawberries**	¾ **cup light rum**
	3 **cups ice cubes**
1 **6-ounce can frozen daiquiri mix**	

Thaw strawberries enough to cut into cubes. Place in blender along with daiquiri mix and rum. Cover and whirl until blended. Add ice cubes, a few at a time, blending until ice is crushed. Pour into shallow pan or ½-gallon freezer container. Cover and freeze several hours or overnight.

To serve, spoon into cocktail or sherbet glasses. Garnish with whole strawberries. Store any unused portion in covered container in freezer. Makes 5 cups.

In 1905, there was a party for Hubbell to celebrate the fiftieth anniversary of his arrival in Des Moines. In 1912, on Hubbell's seventy-third birthday, there was an even bigger party at Terrace Hill. In 1922, on Hubbell's eighty-third birthday, there was a stag party at Terrace Hill. Hubbell said that if he had retired at age seventy, as some prominent men were doing, he might not have lived to be eighty-three. "Idleness kills" was the gist of his wisdom.

PEACH SLUSH

Pink lemonade and well-ripened peaches make this an especially delicious and pretty summer treat. In the winter, use frozen peaches, partially thawed.

1 6-ounce can lemonade concentrate	2 fresh peaches, skinned and sliced
1 6-ounce can vodka	8 to 10 ice cubes

Place all ingredients in blender. Blend until well mixed. Serve immediately in stemmed wine glasses, or store in freezer until ready to serve.

FROZEN SUMMER SLUSH

Perfect for lazy-day summer brunch.

1 6-ounce can frozen lemonade concentrate	1 can water
1 can orange juice	1 can bourbon or vodka

Combine all ingredients. Pour into 1-quart freezer container. Freeze overnight. Spoon into champagne glasses. Makes 6 to 8 servings.

ORANGE JULIUS

Lovely in huge, over-sized wine glasses.

1 6-ounce can frozen orange juice concentrate	½ cup water
½ cup milk	½ teaspoon vanilla
	5 or 6 ice cubes

Blend all ingredients in blender. Makes 8 servings.

KIR

This continental aperitif has a lovely color and delicious flavor.

Creme de cassis
Chablis or other dry white wine, chilled

Pour 1 ounce creme de cassis into each wine glass. Fill with chilled white wine.

CHAMPAGNE COCKTAILS

1 orange	**2 ounces (¼ cup) cognac**
2 lumps sugar	**2 bottles chilled champagne**
Angostura bitters	

Cut the peel from 1 orange into spiral strips. Moisten sugar with bitters. In a large pitcher combine orange peel, crushed sugar, and cognac. Pour in champagne. Strain and serve in chilled champagne glasses. Makes 12 servings.

KAHLUA

5⅓ cups water	**1 quart vodka**
4 cups sugar	**4 teaspoons vanilla**
14 teaspoons instant coffee	**1 cup creme de cocoa**

Simmer the water, sugar and coffee for ½ hour and cool. Add the vodka, vanilla and creme de cocoa. Serve in liqueur glasses for after dinner, or pour over ice cream.

WASSAIL

Winter's chill will be banished by this hot and spicy welcoming Wassail.

3 6-inch cinnamon sticks	18 cups apple cider
3 teaspoons whole allspice	6 cups cranberry juice
48 whole cloves	¾ cup sugar
Peel from 3 oranges, cut up	3 teaspoons butter
Juice of 3 oranges	2 to 3 cups rum

Place the cinnamon sticks, allspice, cloves and orange peel in a cheesecloth bag or percolator basket. In large pan or 30-cup percolator place the orange juice, cider, cranberry juice, sugar and butter. When made in pan, heat until almost boiling. Remove from heat and add rum before serving. Serve hot. In percolator, add rum when cycle is completed. Makes 28 servings. Keeps well in refrigerator for reheating as desired.

HOT CIDER TEA

9 cups tea	9 cups cider
¾ cups sugar	2 to 3 sticks cinnamon

Combine all ingredients, heat and serve. Makes 18 servings.

HOT SPICED WINE

½ gallon port wine	4 to 6 sticks cinnamon
½ gallon Burgandy wine	2 tablespoons whole cloves
1 tablespoon sugar	Peel of 2 oranges and 2 lemons

Combine all ingredients in a large pot and simmer 20 minutes over a very low heat. **Do not boil.**

DINNERS

SAUTEED SLICED BEEF TENDERLOIN

4 pounds tenderloin, sliced about ¼-inch thick	1 cup dry red wine
1 teaspoon salt	1 cup beef broth
Freshly ground pepper	¼ cup olive oil
4 tablespoons flour	Thinly sliced onions and mushrooms (optional)
	¼ cup butter, melted

Remove all fat from meat. Mix salt, pepper and flour in shallow pan and dust each slice of meat lightly. Shake off excess flour. Pour half of butter and oil into a 10 or 12-inch skillet and set over high heat. When pan is hot, add half of meat. Saute no longer than 2 to 3 minutes, turning once. Add a little red wine and cook until it evaporates. Turn into a warmed serving dish and repeat with remaining steak in same pan. Remove and keep meat warm.

Pour beef broth into pan and bring to boil. Scrape and stir to dissolve all dark particles. Add remaining wine and cook about 3 minutes. Add cooked meat only to heat. Do not cook further. (If you wish thicker sauce, add a little arrowroot dissolved in ½ teaspoon lemon juice.) If desired, just before serving add thinly sliced mushrooms and onions. Makes 8 to 10 servings.

BLUE CHEESE SAUCE

¾ cup Maderia wine	6 ounces blue cheese, crumbled
2 tablespoons shallots, minced	
1 cup heavy cream	1 stick unsalted butter, softened
½ cup canned beef broth	

In a saucepan combine the Maderia and shallot and reduce over moderately high heat to about 2 tablespoons. Add the cream and broth and reduce over moderate heat to about 1 cup. Cream the cheese and butter until smooth and whisk, a little at a time, into the saucepan. Simmer for 3 minutes. Strain through a fine sieve and add salt and cayenne to taste. Sprinkle with paprika. Makes about 1½ cups. Especially good over grilled fillet.

BEEF LOBSTER SUPREME

For that extra-special evening when the sky is the limit.

3 to 4 pounds whole beef   2 to 3 lobster tails
     tenderloin   Lemon Butter Sauce

Have the butcher make a pocket in the tenderloin. Choose lobster tails according to size of tenderloin, making sure you have enough to fill the pocket. Cook lobster according to package directions, making sure not to overcook.

Make Lemon Butter Sauce and place cooked lobster in to marinate for approximately 20 minutes, turning several times. Stuff tenderloin with lobster and pour half of sauce over. Bring edges of meat together and tie with string. Pour remaining sauce over meat. Bake, uncovered, in 325° oven for 45 to 60 minutes or until desired doneness.

Lemon Butter Sauce: Melt ¼ pound butter and add the juice of one lemon, strained, ¼ teaspoon salt, ¼ teaspoon pepper, ¼ teaspoon garlic powder and ¼ teaspoon dried basil.

This sauce is also excellent for use over vegetables.

MARINATED TERIYAKI

Tasty steak strips done on the grill will please family and guests.

1 whole flank steak,   ¼ cup chopped green onions
    approximately 1½ pounds   1 clove garlic, minced
1 cup undiluted beef   3 tablespoons lime juice
    consomme   2 tablespoons brown sugar or
½ cup soy sauce   honey
1½ teaspoon seasoned salt

Slice meat into ½-inch thick strips, cutting diagonally across the grain. Refrigerate overnight in a marinade made by combining the rest of the ingredients. Drain meat and grill quickly over hot coals about 2 minutes on each side, basting with marinade. Makes 3 to 4 servings.

Flank Steak *(3 to 4 servings)*

1½ pounds flank steak
¼ cup soy sauce
¼ cup red or white wine

Combine soy sauce and wine in shallow dish. Marinate flank steak for an hour or longer in mixture, turning occasionally. For medium rare, broil steak five minutes on each side, basting once with marinade. Let rest for a couple of minutes before slicing in thin slices across the grain. Always salt steak after it is cooked to avoid toughening.

With best wishes, Rosalynn Carter

MINUTE STEAKS ITALIANO

4 minute steaks	1 8-ounce can tomato sauce
2 teaspoons butter or margarine	1 clove garlic, crushed
	½ teaspoon dried basil
	Mozzarella cheese

Brown minute steaks on both sides in butter. Add garlic and basil to tomato sauce and pour over minute steaks. Cover and simmer over very low heat for at least ½ hour. Top each steak with Mozzarella cheese. Cover and allow cheese to melt. Makes 4 servings.

The kitchen at Terrace Hill was located in the basement along with a servants dining area. A dumbwaiter lifted food to the butler's pantry on first floor, adjacent to the dining room. Servants placed the food in warming ovens until they were called to serve the meal.

STEAK BORDELAISE

This very special sauce may be made ahead of time. Refrigerate to store and reheat to serve.

2 tablespoons each very finely diced carrot, onion and celery	Bouquet Garni (parsley sprig, bay leaf and ¼ teaspoon dried thyme)
1½ tablespoons finely diced ham	
2 tablespoons butter	3 to 4 pounds sirloin steak
1½ tablespoons flour	1½ tablespoons butter
1 recipe Refreshed Bouillon	1½ tablespoons oil
1 tablespoon tomato paste	Dry red wine or vermouth
	6 slices white bread

In saucepan, saute carrot, onion and celery with ham in 1½ tablespoons butter for about 10 minutes. Blend flour into vegetables. Stir over moderate heat until flour turns a golden nut brown. Remove from heat and, with whisk, add Refreshed Bouillon, tomato paste and Bouquet Garni. Simmer 1 hour, stirring occasionally. Final consistency should be thick enough to coat a spoon.

Bring steak to room temperature. Cut into small serving-size pieces. Combine 1½ tablespoons butter and 1½ tablespoons oil in large heavy skillet. Heat until foam of butter begins to subside. Saute meat on one side 3 to 4 minutes. Turn and saute other side just until red juices begin to pearl for rare, 2 minutes more for medium. Remove to platter and keep warm.

Pour fat from skillet. Swirl a bit of red wine or dry vermouth in skillet and scrape brown bits with wooden spoon. Add to Bordelaise Sauce.

Cut pieces of bread in half diagonally. Saute or toast. Serve steaks on toast triangles, mask with sauce. Garnish with parsley or watercress. Pass remaining sauce. Makes 6 servings.

Refreshed Bouillon: Combine 3 cups canned bouillon, ¼ cup each minced carrot and onion, 1½ tablespoons minced celery, ½ cup red wine, 2 sprigs parsley, ½ bay leaf, ¼ teaspoon dried thyme and 1½ tablespoons tomato paste and simmer about 20 minutes. Strain through fine sieve.

La Casa Pacifica

BRAISED STEAKS

1 large onion, sliced
2 to 4 Tbsp. corn oil
¼ tsp. thyme
6 beef round steaks (8 oz. each)
Seasoned salt
Flour
1 cup vegetable cocktail juice (V-8)
1 cup beef broth
1½ cups mixed julienne strips of
   carrots, leeks and celery
2 Tbsp. chopped parsley

Serves 6

In a large ovenproof skillet, saute onion in
1 Tablespoon of the oil until golden. Remove
from heat and add thyme. Set aside.

Sprinkle steaks on both sides with seasoned
salt and flour. Heat remaining oil in an
iron skillet and brown steaks on both sides.
Transfer to pan with onions. Pour vegetable
juice and broth over steaks. Cover and
simmer very slowly 1 hour in the oven or on
top of the stove. Turn steaks, sprinkle with
the vegetable julienne and continue to cook
30 minutes longer.

To serve, arrange steaks on a serving platter.
Spoon sauce and vegetables over steaks and
sprinkle with parsley.

MRS. RICHARD NIXON

BOEUF A LA BOURGUIGNON

Very nice for a buffet supper where guests serve themselves.

½	pound lean salt pork	2	cups dry red wine
2½	pounds beef, cut in		Bouquet Garni*
	2-inch cubes	1	pound small white onions
1	tablespoon flour		(fresh or canned)
1	teaspoon salt	1½	tablespoons butter
½	teaspoon pepper	1	pound mushrooms, sliced
2	cloves garlic, minced	¼	cup chopped parsley

Cut up salt pork and cook in kettle or heat-proof casserole. Using fat, brown meat. Sprinkle with flour and continue to brown. Add salt, pepper, garlic, wine and enough water to cover the meat. Bring to boil, add Bouquet. (*Place a sprig of parsley, a bay leaf and a sprig of dried thyme if you have it, between two stalks of celery. Tie into a bundle with kitchen string. The Bouquet is always removed when the cooking period is over.) Bake, covered, in 350° oven 2 hours.

Meanwhile, brown onions in butter and set aside. Saute mushrooms in butter, adding more butter, if necessary. Add onions, mushrooms and parsley to stew and bake until onions are tender. Serve over white and wild rice combination. Makes 6 servings.

BAKED KIBBEE

2	cups fine cracked wheat	1	teaspoon salt
2	pounds lean ground beef	¼	teaspoon pepper
1	onion, finely grated	¾	cup melted butter

Wash cracked wheat several times and soak in cold water for 10 to 15 minutes to soften. Squeeze to remove water and mix with ground meat, grated onion and spices. Moisten hands with cold water and knead mixture with 2 tablespoons cold water to soften. Butter a 13x9x2-inch pan. Again moisten hands with water and spread mixture evenly in pan. Cut in 2-inch squares and pour melted butter evenly over mixture. Bake in middle rack of 425° oven 45 to 50 minutes. Place squares in Pita bread pockets and top with desired fillings, such as: shredded lettuce, tomatoes, cheese, etc. Makes 12 servings.

ORIENTAL BEEF AND ONIONS

Family and guests will quickly adopt this stir-fried beef and onions as their favorite Oriental dish. Nice even when made with less expensive steaks and chucks.

1½	pounds beef	½	teaspoon salt
1	teaspoon baking soda	1	medium onion, chopped
2	tablespoons soy sauce	4	tablespoons oil
1	tablespoon cornstarch	1/8	teaspoon pepper
2	tablespoons oil		Chinese parsley (optional)
1	tablespoon oil		

Cut beef into slices 2 inches long by 1 inch wide by ¼ inch thick. In a medium bowl toss beef slices with soda, and let stand 15 minutes. Mix soy sauce, cornstarch, and 2 tablespoons oil in a small bowl. Toss beef with this mixture, and marinate 10 minutes more. Set marinated beef by stove with all other ingredients, measured and prepared, along with a slotted spoon and a small bowl.

Set wok or skillet over high heat for 30 seconds, swirl in 1 tablespoon oil, add salt, count to 30. Add onion and stir-fry 2 minutes. Remove onion with slotted spoon to bowl. Add 4 tablespoons oil to the wok or skillet and count to 30, add meat and pepper. Add parsley if desired and stir-fry until color turns gray. Return cooked onion to pan and mix well with beef. Turn into serving dish and serve at once. Makes 4 to 6 servings.

An interview with Frances Hubbell on their fiftieth wedding anniversary in 1913 brought these views: "Why is dress so necessary to women? Why if a gown is good should it be cast aside because it is not the latest dictate of fashion? Where is all this going to lead? Now please do not misunderstand me. I would always want pretty things for my home, but that is what puzzles me, why is not the home and the adornment of the home woman's chief interest? It seems to me woman has branched out into so many avenues. When I was married my first thought was that we should live so that we would always have a good home, and something to keep us, and always my home has seemed to me the important issue."

ZUCCHINI LASAGNE

You'd never know that this flavorful lasagne fits into a low-cal diet.

¾ pound ground beef
½ cup chopped onion
1 15-ounce can tomato sauce
½ teaspoon dried oregano
½ teaspoon dried basil
¾ teaspoon salt

1/8 teaspoon pepper
4 medium zucchini
1 cup cottage cheese
1 egg, beaten
½ pound Mozzarella cheese, grated
Parmesan cheese, grated

Cook ground beef and onion in skillet until beef is browned; drain off fat. Add tomato sauce and seasonings. Simmer, uncovered, 10 minutes. Stir occasionally.

Slice zucchini in lengthwise strips slightly less than ¼-inch thick. Arrange half of strips in greased 12x8x2-inch baking dish. Beat cottage cheese with egg; spread over zucchini. Top with half of Mozzarella and half the meat sauce. Layer again with zucchini, Mozzarella and sauce.

Sprinkle generously with Parmesan cheese. Bake, uncovered, in 350° oven 40 to 45 minutes or until hot and bubbly. Let stand 10 minutes. Makes 6 servings.

GRILLED STEAK ROLLS

8 cube beef steaks
½ teaspoon dried marjoram

Garlic salt, seasoned salt, and pepper
About 5 tablespoons firm butter

Sprinkle steaks with seasonings. Cut 8 pieces of butter, each about 2x1/2x1/4-inches. Place one piece on each steak. Roll each steak, turning ends in first to cover butter well. Tie with string. Broil over medium coals, turning often, until steak is browned but rare inside, 10 to 12 minutes. Makes 8 servings.

On the Fourth of July, the Hubbells traditionally had a dinner party. After dark the housemen would shoot off fireworks on the lawn and neighbors would watch the display from the streets.

WILD RICE BEEF CASSEROLE

1 cup wild rice	2 tablespoons soy sauce
2 pounds ground beef	1 10½-ounce can chicken rice
1 medium onion, diced	soup
½ cup celery, diced	1 10½-ounce can mushroom
1 4-ounce can sliced	soup
mushrooms with liquid	1 cup slivered almonds

Cook rice according to package directions. Brown meat; and drain fat. Mix all ingredients together except almonds. Place in 2-quart casserole and bake in 350° oven 30 minutes. Sprinkle top with almonds. Return to oven for additional 30 minutes. Makes 6 servings.

BEEF AND VEGETABLES CHINESE STYLE

1 pound flank steak	1 clove garlic, minced
(partially frozen)	½ cup water
3 tablespoons oil	3 tablespoons soy sauce
½ pound fresh mushrooms,	1 teaspoon beef bouillon granules
sliced	1 6-ounce package frozen pea
1 onion, sliced and	pods
separated into rings	1 pint cherry tomatoes
½ cup bias-cut celery	1 tablespoon cornstarch
½ cup bias-cut carrots	2 tablespoons water

Cut and assemble all ingredients before starting to cook. Cut steak in strips lengthwise 2-inches wide. Then slice meat across grain in thin slices. Brown meat in 12-inch heavy skillet in oil over high heat. Stir frequently. Add mushrooms, onion, celery, garlic, ½ cup water, carrots, soy sauce and bouillon granules. Reduce heat; simmer covered 5 minutes. Add pea pods and tomatoes. Cover and bring to boil. Simmer 3 minutes.

Meanwhile, blend together cornstarch and 2 tablespoons water. Stir into meat mixture. Cook and stir until mixture comes to a boil and thickens. Serve over hot cooked rice. Makes 6 servings.

CAVATELLI

1	16-ounce package shell macaroni	2	4-ounce cans mushrooms, drained
1	pound Italian sausage	2	teaspoons Italian seasoning
1	pound ground beef	2	8-ounce packages shredded
1	48-ounce jar spaghetti sauce		Mozzarella cheese
	4-ounces mild taco sauce		

Boil macaroni for 20 minutes or until tender. Brown sausage, beef and drain off excess fat. Add macaroni, sauces, mushrooms and seasonings. Pour into 2 12x7x2-inch baking dishes. Top with cheese and bake at 400° for 20-30 minutes. Makes 12 to 15 servings.

HAMBURGER CHEESE BAKE

A wonderful casserole for ladies' lunch or informal supper.

2	pounds ground beef	1	8-ounce package cream cheese, softened
1	medium onion, chopped		
2	15-ounce cans tomato sauce	¼	cup sour cream
1	teaspoon sugar	⅓	cup sliced green onions
¾	teaspoon salt	1	cup cream-style cottage cheese
¼	teaspoon garlic salt	¼	cup chopped green pepper
¼	teaspoon pepper	4	cups medium noodles
		⅓	cup tomato juice
		¼	cup grated Parmesan cheese

Brown the ground beef and onion together. Add tomato sauce, sugar, salt, garlic salt and pepper. Mix together in bowl the cream cheese, sour cream, onion, cottage cheese and green pepper. Cook the noodles according to package directions. Place half the noodles in bottom of 12x7x2-inch baking dish and pour half the meat sauce over them. Pour entire cheese mixture over the meat sauce, then repeat noodle and meat layers. Sprinkle with Parmesan cheese and pour tomato juice over all. Bake in 325° oven for 1 hour. Makes 10 servings.

Aerial view, 1977.

MOUSSAKA

An Eastern Mediterranean version of lasagna. Put the accent on the last syllable—Moo-sah-kah.'

3	medium eggplants	¾	cup butter or margarine
2	large onions, diced	¼	cup all-purpose flour
2	pounds ground lamb	2	cups milk
1	clove garlic, minced	2	tablespoons butter or
3	ripe tomatoes		margarine, melted
1	8-ounce can tomato sauce	1½	teaspoons salt
¼	cup chopped parsley		Dash nutmeg
1	tablespoon salt	1	cup Ricotta or cottage cheese
½	teaspoon ground cinnamon	¼	cup grated Parmesan cheese
		3	eggs, beaten

Peel eggplant, slice lengthwise, salt and set aside. Brown onion, meat and garlic. Add tomatoes, skinned and diced, tomato sauce, parsley 1 tablespoon salt and cinnamon. Cook until most of moisture disappears. Brown eggplant slices in ¾ cup butter. In saucepan, blend flour into 2 tablespoons melted butter. Cook 1 minute. Add milk, 1½ teaspoons salt and nutmeg. Stir. Boil 1 minute. Cool slightly. Stir in cheeses and eggs.

Layer eggplant and meat in 13x9x2-inch or larger lasagna baking pan, 2 layers each. Spoon cheese sauce over top. Bake in 375° oven 30 minutes. Place under broiler a few minutes to brown cheese. Let stand 15 minutes before serving. Makes 8 servings.

MARINATED ROAST LEG OF LAMB

Use this marinade for lamb chops, too.

2	cups dry red wine	2	teaspoons salt
½	cup olive oil	1	teaspoon black pepper
	Juice of 2 lemons	1	clove garlic, crushed
2	tablespoons each of chopped	1	bay leaf
	parsley, dried oregano and	1	leg of lamb
	onion flakes		

Combine all ingredients except meat. Marinate meat in roasting pan in refrigerator for 24 hours. Place pan in oven. Roast in 300° oven 25 minutes per pound of meat, basting occasionally. Makes 8 servings, depending on size of leg.

PORK MEDALLIONS

1 **pound pork tenderloin**	⅔ **cup chicken stock**
Lemon pepper	2 **tablespoons dry vermouth or**
Flour	**other dry white wine**
4 **slices bacon**	4 **slices bread for toast beds**
¼ **pound fresh mushrooms**	

Cut pork into 8 slices. Flatten slightly with palm of hand. Sprinkle with lemon pepper. Dredge in flour. Fry bacon in large skillet until almost crisp. Remove and form into curls. Saute pork in remaining drippings until lightly browned. Remove to shallow baking dish.

Slice and saute mushrooms, including 4 or 5 which have been left whole. Set aside. Add stock and vermouth to skillet and rub with wooden spoon to remove all browned bits. Bring to a boil and cook to reduce by half. Pour over pork in baking dish. Add mushrooms. Cover and bake in a 325° oven about 30 minutes or until pork is done and tender.

Meanwhile trim crusts from bread and cut in half to make 8 triangles. Butter bread and saute or toast until golden. Place bread on platter. Top with meat. Thicken pan juices with equal parts of flour creamed with butter, if desired. Garnish with bacon curls and whole mushrooms. Makes 4 servings.

ORANGE CHUTNEY

An exotic companion for ham or roast pork.

1 **12-ounce jar orange**	1 **teaspoon curry powder**
marmalade	2 **tablespoons red wine vinegar**
¼ **cup raisins**	

Heat ingredients in saucepan until raisins are soft and plump, about ten minutes. Serve warm. Makes 1½ cups.

SWEET SOUR PORK ROAST

If sauce becomes too thick, correct by adding a little vinegar and water.

1	4-pound center cut pork loin roast	1	teaspoon seasoned salt
2	cups sugar	4	teaspoons cornstarch
1	cup vinegar	2	tablespoons water
1	cup water	2	teaspoons paprika
2	tablespoons chopped green pepper	1	tablespoon chopped parsley

Put roast in shallow pan and roast at 450° for 30 minutes. Meanwhile, simmer sugar, vinegar, water, green pepper and salt for 5 minutes. Mix cornstarch and water. Add to sauce and cook until thickened. Stir in paprika and parsley.

Transfer roast to deep baking dish and pour sauce over it. Bake at 300° for 2½ hours, basting occasionally. Makes 8 servings.

GRILLED STUFFED IOWA PORK CHOPS

Ask your butcher to cut the pockets for you.

6	Iowa pork chops, 1¼-inches thick	⅓	cup butter, or margarine melted
½	cup chopped mushrooms	1	tablespoon dried parsley flakes
¼	cup chopped green onion	3	tablespoon lemon juice
		1	cup white wine
		1	teaspoon salt

With sharp knife, beginning at the fat side, halve pork chops horizontally to the bone to form a pocket. Fill with mixture of mushrooms and onion. Insert toothpicks to hold pocket together.

Combine butter, parsley, lemon juice, wine and salt. Place pork chops on grill. Cook about 7 minutes on each side, basting frequently with sauce. Check doneness by cutting slit with knife to see if pink color is gone. Makes 6 servings.

SWEET-SOUR PORK

1½   pounds pork shoulder,
    cubed
2   tablespoons cooking oil
¼   cup water
1   15¼-ounce can pineapple
    chunks
2   tablespoons cornstarch

½   teaspoon salt
¼   cup packed brown sugar
⅓   cup vinegar
1   tablespoon soy sauce
¾   cup sliced green pepper
¼   cup thinly sliced onion
Hot cooked rice

Brown pork cubes in hot oil in skillet. Add water and simmer, covered, 1 hour or till tender.

Drain pineapple, reserving juice. Add water, if necessary, to make 1 cup.

Combine cornstarch, salt and brown sugar. Blend in vinegar. Stir in reserved pineapple juice and soy sauce. Cook, stirring constantly, until thickened and bubbly. Drain pork. Pour sauce over hot pork and let stand 10 minutes.

Add green pepper, onion and pineapple chunks. Simmer, covered, 2 to 3 minutes or until vegetables are tender-crisp. Serve over hot cooked rice. Makes 4 to 6 servings.

SUPER PORK CHOPS

8   butterfly pork chops
8   slices onion, ½-inch thick
8   green pepper rings, 1-inch
    thick

2   cups rice cooked in seasoned
    chicken broth
2   10½-ounce cans condensed
    tomato soup, undiluted

Brown chops and place in roasting pan. Put one slice onion and 1 slice green pepper on each chop. Fill pepper rings with rice. Cover each chop with tomato soup and bake uncovered in 325° oven for 1 hour or more. Makes 8 servings.

PORK CHOP TERIYAKI

This savory recipe is from the National Pork Producers Council of Des Moines.

¼	cup lemon juice	1	clove garlic, minced
1	tablespoon chili sauce	6	pork rib or loin chops,
¾	cup soy sauce		cut 1½ inches thick
1	tablespoon packed brown sugar		

Combine first 5 ingredients. Place pork chops in 13x9x2-inch glass baking dish. Cover. Marinate 3 to 6 hours or overnight in refrigerator, turning chops occasionally.

Broil in oven or on grill about 15 to 20 minutes on each side or unti done, brushing occasionally with remaining marinade. Makes 6 servings.

BARBEQUE SAUCE FOR PORK RIBS

This is good on ribs, pork roast and pork chops.

1	cup catsup	½	teaspoon chili powder
1½	cups water	½	teaspoon dry mustard
½	cup honey		Pinch dried oregano
½	cup chopped onion		Salt
¼	cup packed brown sugar		Pepper
3	dashes Worcestershire	½	cup chopped parsley
3	dashes red wine vinegar	½	cup grated Parmesan cheese

Combine all ingredients and heat until boiling. Simmer 20 minutes. Cool and refrigerate.

The Hubbells' youngest son Grover, his wife Anna and their three daughters Frances, Helen Virginia and Mary Belle moved in to Terrace Hill in 1924, joining the now widowed F. M. Hubbell. A major modernization took place, including the installation of an elevator, new heating plant and electrification.

Around 1928 one of the city's first swimming pools was built on the grounds east of the mansion where a pond had been.

GINGERED HAM SLICE

Excellent when done on the grill and accompanied by Hot Deviled Potatoes. Also good indoors in the broiler accompaned by sweet potatoes.

1	fully cooked center cut ham slice, 1 inch thick	1½	teaspoon wine vinegar
½	cup ginger ale	1	teaspoon dry mustard
½	cup orange juice	¼	teaspoon ground ginger
¼	cup packed brown sugar	1/8	teaspoon ground cloves
1	tablespoon salad oil		

Slash fat edge of ham. Combine remaining ingredients; pour over ham in shallow dish. Refrigerate overnight or let stand at room temperature 2 hours, spooning marinade over ham several times. Broil ham slice over low coals about 15 minutes on each side, brushing frequently with marinade. To serve, spoon marinade over ham. Make 6 servings.

IOWA HAM BALLS

1	pound ground ham	1	cup brown sugar, packed
1½	pounds ground pork	1	teaspoon dry mustard
2	cups soft bread crumbs	½	cup vinegar
2	well beaten eggs	½	cup water
1	cup milk	½	cup horseradish sauce
		½	cup heavy cream, whipped

Combine first five ingredients and form into balls larger than golf ball size. Place in 13x9x2-inch pan. Combine brown sugar, mustard, vinegar and water in saucepan and heat until sugar is dissolved. Pour over ham balls. Bake in 325° oven 1 hour, covered, and 1 hour, uncovered.

Serve with horseradish sauce mixed with whipped cream. Makes 10 servings.

MUSHROOM MADEIRA SAUCE

Use with meat or poultry, especially with fillet mignon.

1 pound fresh mushrooms	1 shallot, finely chopped
4 tablespoons butter	⅓ cup Madeira or dry sherry
½ teaspoon salt	1 recipe Brown Sauce
Dash pepper	½ teaspoon chopped parsley

Cut off the stems level with the caps from mushrooms and reserve the stems for another use. Clean and dry the caps and cut in thick slices or, if very small, leave them whole. Melt butter in a saucepan and add the mushrooms, salt and pepper and cook, shaking the pan frequently, until the mushrooms are golden brown. Add the shallot, Madeira or sherry and Brown Sauce. Bring to a boil and cook slowly for 5 to 6 minutes. Add chopped parsley. Makes 6 servings.

Brown Sauce: Rub pan with ½ clove garlic. Melt 2 tablespoons butter in pan. Stir in, until blended, 2 tablespoons flour. Stir in 1 cup canned bouillon or 1 or 2 bouillon cubes dissolved in 1 cup boiling water. Bring to a boil, stirring constantly.

SHISH KEBOB MARINADE

An exceptionally flavorful marinade for lamb, beef or chicken.

1½ cup oil	1 teaspoon coarse ground pepper
¾ cup soy sauce	1½ teaspoon dried parsley flakes
¼ cup Worcestershire sauce	2 garlic cloves
2 tablespoons dry mustard	⅓ cup lemon juice
2¼ teaspoons salt	

Blend all ingredients in blender. Marinate your choice of meat and vegetables in sauce.

VEAL AUX PROVINCES

Enjoyed in the provinces and also in town!

2 pounds veal, cut Italian style (very thin scallops)	½ cup all-purpose flour
	3 tablespoons oil
½ cup dry bread crumbs	3 tablespoons butter

Mix bread crumbs and flour and dredge veal in mixture. If time permits, allow meat to rest and dredge again before sauteing. Heat oil in a large skillet. Add butter and brown veal. Add oil and butter as needed for browning. As each slice is browned, transfer it to a flat baking dish large enough to hold all the meat without crowding. When all meat is browned, prepare the sauce.

Sauce: Pour ½ cup sherry or madeira into meat drippings in skillet. Cook down for 1 minute. Add 1 cup brown stock and 1 teaspoon tomato paste. Make a smooth paste of 2 tablespoons flour and 3 tablespoons water. Remove from heat and add thickening to sauce in skillet. Return to heat and allow sauce to come to boil and thicken, stirring constantly. Add ½ cup heavy cream and blend in thoroughly.

Pour half of sauce over the veal to mask it. Bake in 400° oven 10 minutes. Reserve the remainder of sauce to be passed at serving time. Serve around a pyramid of buttered rice. Makes 6 servings.

MEATLESS FRESH TOMATO SAUCE

Use your home grown tomatoes to make this light, flavorful sauce and serve over your favorite pasta.

½ cup chopped onion	1½ teaspoons salt
3 garlic cloves, minced	½ teaspoon dried thyme
2 tablespoons butter, olive oil or cooking oil	½ teaspoon dried marjoram
	¼ teaspoon black pepper
3 pounds tomatoes, peeled, seeded and chopped	1 teaspoon dried basil
	½ cup water

Saute onion and garlic in butter or oil until soft. Add the tomatoes, seasonings, and water. Cook, covered, over low heat until tomatoes are tender. Remove cover and cook one hour or until some of liquid has evaporated and sauce has thickened. Stir occasionally.

Canned whole tomatoes and fresh basil or celery leaves may be used. Add mushrooms if desired. Serve over any pasta.

CHICKEN WATERBURY

This is no small amount of work, but is well worth it and can be done ahead of time. Complete recipe, through browning of rolls in fat, and then refrigerate until time to bake, allowing a few extra minutes baking time. These also make elegant picnic fare served cold with a salad and white wine.

½ cup finely chopped mushrooms	5 ounces Danish Havarti cheese, shredded (1¼ cups)
2 tablespoons butter or margarine	6 or 7 boned whole chicken breasts, split
2 tablespoons all-purpose flour	All-purpose flour
½ cup light cream	2 slightly beaten eggs
¼ teaspoon salt	¾ cup fine dry bread crumbs
Dash Cayenne pepper	

Cook mushrooms in butter, about 5 minutes. Blend in flour, stir in cream. Add seasonings; cook and stir until mixture is very thick. Stir in cheese; cook over very low heat, stirring, until cheese melts. Turn into pie plate. Cover. Chill 1 hour. Cut firm cheese mixture into 6 or 7 pieces. Shape into short sticks.

Remove skin from chicken breasts. Place each piece, boned side up, between clear plastic wrap. (Overlap meat where split.) Pound out from center with wood mallet to form cutlets not quite ¼-inch thick. Peel off wrap. Sprinkle meat with salt. Place a cheese stick on each piece. Tucking in the sides, roll as for jellyroll. Press to seal well. Dust rolls with flour; dip in egg, then in crumbs. Cover and chill thoroughly—at least 1 hour.

An hour before serving, fry rolls in deep, hot fat (375°) for 5 minutes or until golden brown. Drain on paper towels. Bake in shallow baking pan, 7x11x1½-inches, in 325° oven 30 to 45 minutes. Makes 6 or 7 servings.

On March 19, 1924 the Hubbells celebrated their sixty-first wedding anniversary with a party at Terrace Hill. Frances Hubbell was eighty-three years old. Guests were received from 3 p.m. to 6 p.m. in the east living room, which was filled with baskets of flowers. Frances' sister Florence Cooper Ginn attended—she had also been at the wedding in 1863. Two months later Frances died.

RUBY CHICKEN

Chicken breasts in a tangy sweet-sour sauce.

10 chicken breasts, skinned
1 16-ounce can whole cranberry sauce

1 package dried onion soup mix
1 8-ounce bottle Russian dressing

Place chicken breasts in single layer in 13x9x2-inch baking dish. Mix the cranberries, soup mix and dressing together and pour over chicken. Marinate overnight. Bake in 350° oven for 1 to 2 hours or until chicken is done. Makes 10 servings.

CHICKEN BREASTS WITH BLACK CHERRIES

3 chicken breasts, halved
6 tablespoons butter or margarine
1 cup port wine
½ cup chicken broth

2 teaspoons maggi seasoning
1 tablespoon cornstarch
2 tablespoons water
1 cup pitted black cherries

Brown breasts in butter in skillet. Arrange in 8x8x2-inch baking dish. Cover and bake in 350° oven 20 minutes. Meanwhile, add port, broth and maggi seasoning to the skillet. Stir well and simmer 10 minutes. Dissolve cornstarch in water; stir into skillet and simmer until the sauce is clear, stirring constantly. Add cherries. Pour over chicken. Cover casserole and continue baking 20 minutes. Makes 6 servings.

CHICKEN WORTHY OF TERRACE HILL

Mrs. Richard Ingham sent us this current favorite recipe, along with the personal comments below:

½	cup sour cream	1	teaspoon salt
1	tablespoon lemon juice	Dash pepper	
1	teaspoon Worcestershire sauce	1	2-to 2½-pound chicken,
1	teaspoon celery salt		quartered
½	teaspoon paprika	1	cup dry bread crumbs
2	cloves garlic, minced		

Mix together all ingredients except chicken and bread crumbs. Dip chicken into mixture and then roll in bread crumbs. Bake in 13x9x2-inch baking pan in 350° oven 45 to 60 minutes or until chicken is tender and surface is crusty brown. Makes 3 servings.

My memories of Terrace Hill are those of a nine or ten-year-old. Sometimes at Christmas, sometimes at Thanksgiving, about thirty-five Hubbells and Thompsons assembled as guests of Mr. and Mrs. Grover Hubbell (my great-aunt and uncle).

I remember nothing about the food, but still vivid is the memory's picture of long, beautifully arrayed tables, an abundance of flowers, crystal wine service for each course, candlelight and a gift at each child's place!

Maids attired in snappy black dresses with perky white aprons and pleated white head bands served us soup, salad, wines, dinner and dessert. There was no need for parental coaching, for we children sensed that this was an occasion for careful eating and best manners.

Helen Ann Hubbell Ingham
(Mrs. Richard Schuyler Ingham)

CHICKEN SALTIMBOCCA

3 large chicken breasts, skinned
   boned and halved lengthwise
6 thin slices boiled ham
3 slices Mozarella cheese,
   halved
1 large tomato, chopped

½ teaspoon dried sage, crushed
⅓ cup fine dry bread crumbs
2 tablespoons grated Parmesan
   cheese
2 tablespoons snipped parsley
4 tablespoons melted butter or
   margarine

Place chicken boned side up on cutting board. Cover with a sheet of plastic wrap. Working from center out, pound lightly with meat mallet to approximately 5 x 5-inch pieces. Remove wrap. Place a ham slice and half slice cheese on each cutlet, cutting to fit. Top with a spoonful of tomato and a dash of sage. Tuck in sides; roll jelly roll style, pressing to seal well. Combine bread crumbs, Parmesan and parsley. Dip chicken in butter, then roll in crumbs and place in shallow pan. Bake in 350° oven 40 to 45 minutes. Makes 6 servings.

GRAND AVENUE PARTY CHICKEN

6 slices bacon
3 whole chicken breasts, split,
   boned and skinned
¼ cup water
1 3-ounce package sliced
   smoked beef

1 can condensed cream of
   onion soup
½ cup dairy sour cream
1 tablespoon flour
Paprika

Cook bacon until crisp. Remove, crumble and reserve. Drain bacon drippings; discard. Place chicken breasts and water in same skillet. Cover and simmer 10 minutes. Pour off water. Fold six slices of beef in half and wrap around each breast. Return chicken to skillet.

Combine soup, sour cream and flour. Cut up remaining smoked beef and add to sour cream mixture. Spoon over chicken in skillet. Sprinkle with paprika. Simmer, covered, 8 minutes or until hot. Serve garnished with bacon. Makes 6 servings.

LEMON SOY GRILLED CHICKEN

2 broiler chickens, halved	⅓ cup lemon juice
⅓ cup soy sauce	⅓ cup cooking oil

Place chicken halves in large shallow pan. Combine remaining ingredients. Pour over chicken. Let stand at room temperature 1 hour, turning chicken frequently. Cook on grill, turning and basting. Makes 4 to 6 servings.

HONEY DIPPED BARBEQUED CHICKEN

3 2½ to 3 pound broiler fryer chickens, quartered	2 tablespoons prepared mustard
Salt and pepper	½ cup dry white wine
1 cup soy sauce	½ cup honey
1 cup catsup	1 teaspoon ground ginger

Sprinkle chicken on all sides with salt and pepper. In oblong dish mix remaining ingredients, stirring until blended. Add chicken. Marinate for several hours or overnight in the refrigerator. Turn occasionally. Drain chicken and reserve marinade. Place skin side up on grill rack 8 inches above medium hot coals. Grill 50 to 60 minutes, turning and basting every 10 minutes. Makes 10 to 12 servings.

Memories later recalled by Elmer Nelson, chauffeur, butler, gardener, et cetera for the Hubbells for thirty-three years, made it seem as if there were always parties at Terrace Hill in the twenties and thirties. Mr. Nelson's daughter recalls, ''The summer was our favorite, for the Hubbells had several hundred guests and they were served from tables that were gorgeous, with ice images carved with colored lights below them for centerpieces. They were a sight to see. They would bring in portable dance floors, hire orchestras, and dance until the wee hours of the morning.''

CHICKEN TETRAZZINI

Outstanding flavor in this do-ahead casserole for easy, elegant entertaining.

5 pound roasting chicken or	2 onions, sliced
2 2½-pound broiler-	4 carrots, sliced
fryers, cut up	3 stalks celery, chopped
4 cups hot water	1½ teaspoons onion salt
2½ teaspoons salt	1 teaspoon celery seed
	1 teaspoon poultry seasoning

Simmer all ingredients together until chicken is cooked 45 to 60 minutes. Cool and remove meat in large pieces. Puree vegetables and add enough stock to make 2 cups and set aside. Add rest of stock to enough water to make 6 quarts and season with 3 tablespoons salt. Bring to a boil and add 1¼ pounds spaghettini. Cook 6 minutes. Drain, place in bottom of 13x9x2-inch baking dish.

4 tablespoons butter or	1½ tablespoons lemon juice
margarine	¾ teaspoon salt
¾ pound mushrooms, sliced	½ cup sliced almonds

Melt butter or margarine in skillet and saute mushrooms. Sprinkle with lemon juice, salt and sliced almonds. Pour mixture over spaghettini.

4 tablespoons butter or	1/8 teaspoon ground nutmeg
margarine	¼ cup dry sherry
2 tablespoons flour	2 cups reserved chicken broth
¼ teaspoon paprika	with vegetables
1½ teaspoons salt	1 cup heavy cream
½ teaspoon pepper	

Melt the butter or margarine and blend in the flour, paprika, salt, pepper, and nutmeg, stirring constantly. Slowly stir in the sherry and chicken broth. Cook and stir until thickened. Remove from heat and add the heavy cream. Mix this sauce with the chicken and pour on top of spaghettini and mushrooms and almonds. Refrigerate or freeze if desired. When ready to serve bring to room temperature, sprinkle with 1 cup grated parmesan cheese and paprika. Bake in 350° oven for ½ to ¾ hour. Makes 8 servings.

THREE CHEESE CHICKEN BAKE

8 ounces lasagna noodles	½ cup grated Parmesan cheese
3 cups diced, cooked chicken	8 ounces process American
1½ cups cream-style cottage	cheese, shredded
cheese	Mushroom Sauce

Cook lasagna noodles according to package directions. Rinse in cold water and drain. Place half the noodles in bottom of greased 13x9x2-inch baking dish. Cover with half of each: mushroom sauce, cottage cheese, chicken, Parmesan cheese and process cheese. Repeat layers. Bake in 350° oven for 45 minutes. Makes 8 to 10 servings.

Mushroom Sauce: Melt 3 tablespoons butter and saute ½ cup chopped onion and ½ cup chopped green pepper. Add 1 10½-ounce can condensed cream of chicken soup, ⅓ cup milk, 1 6-ounce can sliced mushrooms, drained; ¼ cup chopped pimiento and ½ teaspoon basil. Cook and stir until smooth. Makes 8 to 10 servings.

COMPANY CHICKEN CACCIATORE

Tender crisp vegetables and chicken breasts make this company fare.

4 whole chicken breasts, split, boned and skinned	2 medium tomatoes, skinned and chopped
3 tablespoons cooking oil	¾ cup tomato puree
1 medium onion, sliced	¾ cup dry red wine
½ small green pepper, seeded and sliced	1 teaspoon salt
1 pound fresh mushrooms	½ teaspoon dried oregano
2 cloves garlic, minced	¼ teaspoon pepper

Brown chicken in hot oil in skillet. Remove chicken from skillet. Add onion, green pepper, mushrooms and garlic to skillet and cook until vegetables are tender crisp. Remove and set aside.

Return chicken to skillet. Stir in remaining ingredients. Simmer, covered, 45 minutes or until chicken is tender. Remove chicken and keep warm. Cook sauce over high heat until thick, stirring frequently. Return chicken and vegetables to sauce. Makes 4 servings.

CHICKEN DIVAN

Serve this at your next dinner party. Your friends will call it divine.

2	10-ounce packages frozen broccoli spears	½	cup grated Parmesan cheese
1	10¾-ounce can condensed cream of chicken soup	2	cups sliced cooked chicken
		½	cup whipping cream
1	teaspoon Worcestershire sauce	½	cup mayonnaise or salad dressing
1/8	teaspoon ground nutmeg		

Cook broccoli according to package directions, drain. Arrange in 12x7½x2-inch baking dish. Blend soup, Worcestershire and nutmeg. Pour half over vegetable. Sprinkle with ⅓ of the cheese. Top with chicken and remaining soup mixture. Sprinkle with another ⅓ of the cheese. Bake, uncovered in 350° oven until heated through, about 20 minutes. Whip cream until soft peaks form; fold in mayonnaise. Spead mixture over chicken. Sprinkle with remaining cheese. Broil 3 to 4 inches from heat till golden, 1 to 2 minutes. Makes 6 servings.

West view of Terrace Hill and private entrance.

STUFFED DUCK BORDELAISE—Mrs. Gerald R. Ford

2	4½ to 5 pound ducks	**Stuffing:**
	Salt and pepper	2 tablespoons butter
1	pound mushrooms, sliced	4 tablespoons shallots, finely
2	carrots, coarsely chopped	chopped
2	sticks celery, coarsely	**Duck livers, chopped**
	chopped	1 tablespoon parsley, chopped
1	bay leaf	8 green olives, chopped
	Pinch of rosemary	**Sage**
2	cups chicken stock	**Thyme**
1	cup dry white wine	**Grated nutmeg**
2	tablespoons Madeira wine	**Salt and pepper**
		4 slices bread, finely diced
		2 eggs

Stuff ducks, tie with string and season with salt and pepper. Brown them on both sides in a roasting pan over medium heat. Add mushrooms, carrots, celery, bay leaf, rosemary, chicken stock and white wine. Cover and bake in a preheated 350° oven for 1 to 1½ hours. Remove ducks from roasting pan and strain the pan juices. Remove the fat from the juices. Boil juices until they are reduced to 2½ cups. Add Madeira wine and bring to a boil. Cut duck into pieces and arrange on large serving platter. Serve hot juices separately. Makes 6 servings.

Stuffing: Melt butter in saucepan, add shallots and simmer for 2 minutes. Add livers and saute for 2 additional minutes. Add remaining ingredients except the bread and eggs. Remove from heat and add the bread, mixing well with a rubber spatula. Add eggs, 1 at a time, mixing well after each addition.

GOURMET PHEASANT

Breasts and legs of 4
   pheasants
¼   cup butter
1   cup brandy
2   cups chicken stock
1   onion, chopped

1   clove garlic, minced
Salt and pepper, to taste
1   quart (or less) half and half
1   5-ounce bottle horseradish
½   pound fresh mushrooms,
   sauteed in butter
Hot cooked rice

Brown pheasant in butter. Place in deep baking dish or Dutch oven and pour the brandy over. Ignite brandy and let flame burn out. Add chicken stock, onion and garlic. Season with salt and pepper. Bake in 350° oven for ½ hour, basting several times. Remove dish from oven and pour over the heavy cream mixed with horseradish. Replace in oven and bake 1½ hours. Ten minutes before serving, add sauteed mushrooms. Serve with rice. Makes 8 servings.

SMOKED TURKEY WITH WINE SAUCE

We predict you'll use a spoon to eat up the last drop of the sauce!

1   pound margarine
1   cup lemon juice
1   cup Worcestershire or soy
   sauce or combination
1   tablespoon salt
1   tablespoon paprika

1   teaspoon monosodium
   glutamate
Dash Tabasco sauce
½   cup sherry
1½   cups dry white wine
10 - 14 pound turkey

Combine first 7 ingredients in saucepan and bring to boil. Remove from heat and add sherry; mix well. Pour white wine into cavity of turkey in foil roasting pan. Add handful of dampened hickory chips to charcoal fire. Place turkey on grill and cover with grill lid. Baste frequently with sauce. Cook 2 to 6 hours, depending on size of turkey and grill. (Rotisserie may be used.) Serve remaining sauce with turkey.

ROLLED FILLET OF SOLE FILLED WITH CRAB MEAT

4 or 8 fillets of sole,
depending on size
½ pound crab meat, picked
over to remove shell particles
2 tablespoons butter or
margarine, melted
2 teaspoons shallots or onions,
finely chopped

4 ounces champagne or dry
white wine
½ cup heavy cream
Juice of one-half lemon
2 egg yolks
¼ cup heavy cream
½ teaspoon cornstarch
1 tablespoon water

Rinse fillets, spread out flat and cover each with a layer of crab meat. Roll and fasten with a toothpick. Pour 2 tablespoons melted butter in 8x8x2-inch dish. Place fillets in dish side by side and sprinkle shallots over. Pour wine, ½ cup cream and lemon juice over and bake in 375° oven 10 minutes. Transfer to a serving dish and keep warm.

Beat egg yolks slightly with ¼ cup cream. Add the wine in which fish have been baking. Dissolve cornstarch in water and add to sauce. Put fillets back into baking dish. Pour sauce over them and return to oven for 10 minutes. Makes 4 servings.

FISH FILLETS IN MUSHROOM—MORNAY SAUCE

3 tablespoons butter or
margarine
3 tablespoons flour
1 10¾-ounce can cream of
mushroom soup

½ cup dry white wine
2 tablespoons grated Parmesan
cheese
2 tablespoons chopped parsley
1 to 2 pounds fish fillets (sole,
cod, halibut)

Melt butter and stir in flour. Add soup and wine and cook, stirring until mixture boils and thickens. Add cheese and parsley. Arrange fillets in single layer in greased 13x9x2-inch baking dish. Pour sauce over fish. Bake in 375° oven about 25 minutes until fish flakes when tested with fork. Makes 4 to 6 servings.

BAKED HADDOCK IN CUSTARD SAUCE

1 tablespoon butter or margarine	¼ teaspoon dry mustard
	1 teaspoon salt
2 pounds haddock fillets, cut in 6 serving pieces	1/8 teaspoon pepper
	1¼ cups milk
½ cup finely chopped onions	2 eggs
½ teaspoon Worcestershire sauce	1 cup crushed cornflakes

Melt the butter or margarine in an 8x8x2-inch casserole in oven. Place the fish and onion in the dish. Stir the Worcestershire, mustard, salt, and pepper into the milk. Pour half the mixture over the fish and place in preheated 400° oven. Bake 30 minutes. In the meantime beat the eggs into the remaining milk. Pour over the baked fish, sprinkle with crushed cornflakes and return to hot oven. Turn off heat and leave in oven for 15 to 20 minutes or until a custard forms. Makes 6 servings.

BARBECUED SHRIMP

1 pound uncooked medium sized shrimp	1 tablespoon cider vinegar
	½ teaspoon ground ginger
¼ cup soy sauce	Dash cayenne pepper
2 tablespoons tomato juice	2 teaspoons sugar
1 tablespoon water	1 clove garlic, minced

Peel and devein shrimp. Thread 6 shrimp on each of 4 skewers. Place on broiler pan.

In small saucepan combine remaining ingredients. Heat to boiling. Reduce heat and simmer 3 minutes, uncovered.

Brush shrimp thoroughly with sauce. Broil 4 inches from heat for 2 minutes on each side or until tender. Brush frequently with sauce. May be cooked on grill. Makes 4 servings.

ASPARAGUS SPOON BREAD

2¼ cups milk
½ cup white or yellow
   cornmeal
1½ teaspoon baking powder
1¼ teaspoons salt
1 teaspoon sugar

1 tablespoon butter or
   margarine
2 cups shredded cheddar cheese
4 eggs, separated
3 cups cooked asparagus, cut
   into ½ inch pieces

Preheat oven to 375°. Grease a 2 quart casserole or souffle dish. Cook milk and cornmeal over medium high heat, stirring constantly, until very soft and thickened, 2-3 minutes. Remove from heat and add next five ingredients. Beat with whisk until cheese is melted and mixture is cool. Stir in yolks one at a time. Beat egg whites until stiff. Fold into yolk mixture. Fold in asparagus. Bake 45-50 minutes. Center should not quiver when dish is shaken. Serve at once. Makes 6 to 8 servings.

ASPARAGUS WITH YOGURT DRESSING

A low-calorie salad or vegetable with a lovely, tangy dressing.

1 10-ounce package frozen
   asparagus spears
1 small head Boston or bibb
   lettuce
½ cup plain yogurt

1 small clove garlic, crushed
1 tablespoon chopped parsley
¼ teaspoon salt
1 hard-cooked egg yolk
Freshly ground pepper

Cook asparagus, following label instructions; drain well on paper toweling. Cool; chill. Just before serving, arrange asparagus on lettuce leaves. Combine yogurt, garlic, parsley and salt in measuring cup. Spoon over asparagus; save remainder of sauce to pass at the table. Press the egg yolk through seive. Sprinkle over yogurt and serve with freshly ground pepper. Makes 4 servings.

ARTICHOKE HEARTS SURPRISE

2 9-ounce packages frozen
   artichoke hearts
1 tablespoon lemon juice
1 tablespoon butter or
   margarine
¼ teaspoon salt

¼ teaspoon pepper
1 10-ounce package frozen
   chopped broccoli
1 medium onion, chopped
1 recipe White Sauce
2 tablespoons grated Parmesan
   cheese

Cook artichokes in boiling, salted water until barely tender; drain. Season with lemon juice, butter, salt and pepper and place in greased 1-quart casserole. Cook broccoli and onion in boiling, salted water until tender; drain. Puree in blender, food processor or put through food mill. Combine broccoli puree, white sauce and cheese. Season with salt and pepper, if necessary. Pour over artichokes. Bake in 375° oven 10 minutes. May be made a day in advance and refrigerated. If so, bake 15 minutes. Makes 6 servings.

White Sauce: Melt 2 tablespoons butter or margarine in small saucepan. Blend in 2 tablespoons flour, ¼ teaspoon salt and dash pepper. When mixture is bubbly, blend in 1 cup milk. Cook, stirring constantly, until mixture thickens and boils.

BRUSSELS SPROUTS CASSEROLE

Elegant treatment for this vegetable.

2 10-ounce packages frozen
   Brussels sprouts
½ cup chopped pecans
¼ cup flour
½ cup powdered non-dairy
   creamer
¼ teaspoon ground nutmeg

2 tablespoons butter or
   margarine
1 cup boiling chicken broth
1 cup seasoned stuffing mix
2 tablespoons butter or
   margarine, melted

Put Brussels sprouts and nuts in greased 1½-quart casserole. Combine flour, non-dairy creamer and nutmeg. Sprinkle over vegetables. Dot with 2 tablespoons butter and pour on boiling broth. Bake, covered in 350° oven 15 minutes. Stir and continue baking 15 minutes longer. Sprinkle stuffing mix over top. Dot with 2 tablespoons butter. Continue baking, uncovered, 10 minutes. Makes 6 to 8 servings.

BAKED BEANS

1 large onion, chopped	1 tablespoon packed brown
½ pound ground beef	sugar
3 16-ounce cans baked beans,	2 tablespoons liquid smoke
partially drained	½ cup catsup

Cook onion and ground beef in skillet until beef is browned. Combine with beans, brown sugar, liquid smoke and catsup. Place in a 2-quart casserole. Bake in a 350° oven 45 minutes or until bubbly. Makes 8 servings.

HERBED GREEN BEANS

Add spice to your green beans.

3 tablespoons butter or	1 10-ounce package frozen
margarine	green beans
¼ teaspoon celery seed	Garlic salt to taste
¼ teaspoon dried basil	Salt and pepper to taste
¼ teaspoon ground Rosemary	1 tablespoon instant minced
1 tablespoon chopped parsley	onion

Combine butter, celery seed, basil, rosemary, parsley and instant minced onion in small skillet. Cook over low heat 10 minutes.

Meanwhile cook green beans as directed on package; drain. Add butter mixture. Season to taste with garlic salt, salt and pepper. Makes 3 servings.

COMPANY CARROTS

4 tablespoons butter or	8 carrots, cut in small sticks,
margarine	cooked and drained
1 tablespoon minced onion	½ teaspoon salt
½ cup stuffed green olives,	½ teaspoon sugar
sliced	Dash freshly ground pepper

Melt butter in skillet; add onion and cook just until tender. Add olives and carrots; season with salt, sugar and pepper. Shake over medium high heat until heated through. Makes 6 to 8 servings.

ORANGE GLAZED CARROTS

2 pounds carrots	½ teaspoon salt
1 tablespoon sugar	¾ cup orange juice
2 teaspoons cornstarch	

Cut carrots in 2-inch lengths. Cook in boiling, salted water until just tender; drain.

Combine sugar, cornstarch and salt in saucepan. Blend in orange juice. Cook over medium heat, stirring constantly, until mixture thickens and bubbles. Add cooked carrots to sauce. Heat 3 minutes. Makes 6 to 8 servings.

CELERY CASSEROLE

4 cups celery, cut in 1-inch pieces	1 10½-ounce can condensed cream of chicken soup
1 cup water chestnuts, sliced	¼ cup soft bread crumbs
¼ cup chopped pimiento	¼ cup toasted, slivered
½ cup chopped green pepper	almonds
	2 tablespoons butter or margarine

Combine celery, water chestnuts, pimiento, green pepper and chicken soup. Spoon into a greased 1-quart casserole. Toss together bread crumbs, almonds and melted butter. Sprinkle over top. Bake in 350° oven 55 minutes. Makes 6 to 8 servings.

SPINACH-STUFFED MUSHROOMS

1 12-ounce package frozen spinach souffle, thawed	½ teaspoon fresh lemon juice
	Dash hot pepper sauce
⅓ cup packaged seasoned breadcrumbs	18 to 20 large fresh mushrooms
⅓ cup grated Parmesan cheese	⅓ cup melted butter or margarine

Combine spinach souffle, breadcrumbs, Parmesan cheese, lemon juice and hot pepper sauce; mix well. Wash mushrooms; remove stems and save for another use. Dip mushrooms in melted butter; place in a shallow baking dish. Spoon spinach mixture atop mushrooms, rounding top of each. Drizzle with remaining butter. Bake at 400° about 15 to 20 minutes or until souffle mixture is puffed and done. Makes 18 to 20.

DEVILED MUSHROOMS

Excellent as a first course or as an accompaniment to beef or chicken.

1 pound mushrooms	½ teaspoon tabasco sauce
¼ cup butter	2 teaspoons Worcestershire sauce
3 tablespoons oil	1 tablespoon fresh lemon juice
½ teaspoon salt	1 clove garlic, minced
¼ teaspoon pepper	1 teaspoon fresh minced chervil
	or ½ teaspoon dried

Saute the mushrooms in butter and oil, shaking pan as for popcorn. Season with salt and pepper. Add the remaining ingredients. Cook for 1 to 3 minutes. Taste for seasoning and serve with crisp crusted bread in small ramekins as a first course or pass as a meat accompaniment. Makes 3 to 4 servings.

MUSHROOMS MADEIRA

2 pounds fresh mushrooms	2 green onions, chopped
¼ cup butter or margarine	½ cup Madeira or sherry
¾ teaspoon salt	1 tablespoon chopped parsley
¼ teaspoon pepper	2 tablespoons cornstarch
	½ cup cold water

Clean mushrooms. Melt butter in skillet; add mushrooms, salt and pepper and saute until golden brown. Add green onions, wine and parsley. Bring to boil and simmer for 5 minutes. Blend water and cornstarch. Stir into mushroom mixture. Bring to boil, stirring constantly. Simmer 2 to 3 minutes. Place in 1½ quart casserole and bake in 325° oven 15 minutes. Makes 6 to 8 servings.

FRENCH ONION CASSEROLE

This is delicious and different—like the best part of onion soup.

4	to 6 medium onions, sliced	¼	cup sherry
3	tablespoons butter or margarine	1½	cups croutons
2	tablespoons flour	2	tablespoons melted butter or margarine
Dash pepper		3	tablespoons grated Parmesan cheese
¾	cup beef bouillon	½	cup grated Swiss cheese

Saute onions in butter in skillet until just tender. Blend in flour and pepper. Add bouillon and sherry. Cook and stire until thick and bubbly. Toss croutons with 2 tablespoons butter. Spoon into 8x8x2-inch pan. Pour on onion mixture and sprinkle with Swiss and Parmesan cheese. Place under broiler until cheese melts, 2 to 3 minutes. Serve immediately. Makes 4 to 6 servings.

SWEET AND SOUR PEARL ONIONS

Serve these flavorful onions as a garnish with any meat.

¼	cup bacon fat	⅓	cup sherry
2	tablespoons butter	Salt to taste	
½	pound pearl onions, peeled	1½	tablespoons brown sugar
⅓	cup white wine vinegar		

In a saucepan heat the bacon fat with the butter. Add the onions, vinegar, sherry and salt. Cover the pan and cook 25-35 minutes over low heat or until they are tender but not brown, stirring occasionally. Add the brown sugar and cook the onions uncovered for a few minutes longer or until the liquid is reduced and the onions are glazed. Makes 4 to 6 servings.

When fresh pearl onions are unobtainable, canned ones may be used. Cook the sauce to blend the flavors and add the onions to marinate for 30 minutes, then heat through.

PEAS AND ONIONS PAPRIKA

An elegant vegetable combination for entertaining. Tastes as good as it looks. Can be prepared a day ahead.

3 large onions, cut in half crosswise	1 tablespoon cornstarch
Paprika	1 16-ounce can peas
¼ cup chopped onion	2 tablespoons chopped pimiento
2 tablespoons butter or margarine	¼ teaspoon salt
	¼ teaspoon Worcestershire sauce

Remove centers from onion halves; place onion shells in baking dish and cover with foil. Bake in 375° oven for 20 minutes. Sprinkle top of onion cups with paprika. Chop enough onion centers to make ¼ cup. Saute chopped onion in butter or margarine until tender. Drain peas, reserving liquid. Blend in cornstarch and liquid drained from peas. Cook stirring constantly until thickened. Add peas, pimiento and seasonings, mix well. Fill onion cups with mixture. Cover with foil and bake in 375° oven for 15 minutes. Makes 6 servings.

SPINACH SOUR CREAM PUFF

1 10-ounce package frozen chopped spinach	1 cup grated Parmesan cheese
1 tablespoon grated onion	1 tablespoon flour
2 eggs	2 tablespoons butter or margarine
½ cup sour cream	Salt and pepper to taste

Cook spinach in small amount of water with onion until thawed. Drain thoroughly. Beat eggs; add remaining ingredients and spinach. Bake in greased 1-quart casserole in 350° oven for 25 to 30 minutes until center is set. Do not overcook, as it will separate. Makes 4 servings.

PENNSYLVANIA DUTCH TOMATOES

These are excellent dished up on toast and accompanied with fried bacon strips.

2 medium size firm tomatoes, ripe or green	2 tablespoons butter or bacon fat
½ cup flour	½ cup packed brown sugar
	Heavy cream

Cut tomatoes in thick slices and dip in flour. Saute in butter or bacon fat and before turning sprinkle the top side with brown sugar. Then turn and let the sugar melt into the fat and brown. Sprinkle with a little more sugar and let it melt down on top. Pour in enough heavy cream to just cover tomato slices and let come to a boil and thicken. Serve immediately. Makes approximately 4 servings.

TURNIP SAUTE

Turnips and confectioners' sugar will surprise you.

6 to 8 medium turnips	2 tablespoons confectioners' sugar
¼ cup butter or margarine	

Remove root and top of turnips. Cut in slices of uniform size and thickness. Cook, covered, in 1 cup boiling, salted water about 15 minutes or until tender. Drain. Just before serving, melt butter in skillet, add turnips. Sprinkle with sugar. Saute until lightly browned, about 5 minutes. Makes 6 servings.

At Christmas the largest tree on the lawn in front of the house would be decorated with lights.

CHEESEY VEGETABLE COMBO

1	10-ounce package frozen chopped broccoli	1	tablespoon butter or margarine
1	10-ounce package frozen cauliflower	1	8-ounce jar processed cheese spread
1	10-ounce package Brussels sprouts	2	to 3 tablespoons Worcestershire sauce
½	cup chopped scallions	¾	cup slivered or sliced toasted almonds

Cook vegetables 3 to 5 minutes in boiling, salted water and drain. Saute scallions in butter. Mix with vegetables and place all in 2-quart casserole. Stir cheese spread and Worcestershire sauce over low heat until melted. Pour over vegetables and sprinkle with almonds. Bake in 350° oven for 30 minutes. Makes 8 servings.

GARDEN VEGETABLE BAKE

A colorful and delicious vegetable combination.

1½	cups thinly-sliced onions	1	16-ounce can tomatoes, undrained and broken up
1½	cups thinly-sliced carrots		
¾	cup coarsely chopped green pepper	2	teaspoons salt
2	cups sliced celery	1/8	teaspoon pepper
2	cups green beans, canned or frozen	3	tablespoons tapioca

Combine ingredients in a 13x9x2-inch glass baking dish. Cover tightly with foil and bake at 350° for 1 hour and 10 minutes. Makes 8 to 10 servings.

GRILLED VEGETABLE TRIO

A fresh tasting and easy vegetable good with any meat.

½	pound carrots, cut into julienne strips	¼	pound mushrooms, sliced
½	pound green beans, cut into 1-inch pieces	1	teaspoon salt
		½	teaspoon dried thyme
		3	tablespoons butter or margarine

Place vegetables on a sheet of heavy duty foil, sprinkle with seasonings and dot with the butter. Seal foil, turning up the ends and securing. Grill over medium coals for 1 hour or until done.

FETTUCINI WITH ZUCCHINI AND MUSHROOMS

An unusual, hearty dish for family or special occasions. So rich you won't miss meat.

½	pound mushrooms, sliced	½	cup butter or margarine
¼	cup butter or margarine	1	pound fettucini
1¼	pounds zucchini, julienned	¾	cup grated Parmesan cheese
1	cup heavy cream	½	cup chopped parsley
		1	teaspoon salt
		¼	teaspoon pepper

In large, deep skillet saute mushrooms in ¼ cup butter over medium high heat for 2 minutes. Add zucchini, cream and ½ cup butter, in bits. Bring to boil and simmer 3 minutes.

Place fettucini in boiling water with 2 tablespoons salt and 1 tablespoon olive oil for 7 minutes. Drain, add to skillet with Parmesan cheese and parsley. Season with salt and pepper. Toss with wooden forks and serve immediately with more Parmesan. Makes 6 servings.

ZUCCHINI RICE CASSEROLE

This combination of fresh vegetables and seasonings never fails to please.

1 large or 2 medium zucchini
  unpeeled and sliced
Salt and pepper
Garlic salt
Ground oregano
⅓ to ¼ cup raw precooked
  rice

2 large tomatoes, sliced
12 to 14 slices process
  American cheese food
1 medium red onion, sliced
  into rings
4 strips uncooked bacon, cut
  into 1-inch pieces

Layer the sliced zucchini in a 13x9x2-inch baking dish. Sprinkle with salt, pepper, garlic salt, oregano, and rice. Then make a layer of sliced tomatoes, a layer of cheese, a layer of onions and sprinkle the bacon pieces over the top. Bake in a 350° oven, tightly covered, for 45 minutes. Uncover and brown for 15 minutes. Makes 8 servings.

ZUCCHINI TOMATO CASSEROLE

Garden fresh vegetables make this a real treat.

¼ cup salad oil
1 small clove garlic
6 small unpeeled zucchini,
  sliced
1½ teaspoons seasoned salt
½ cup shredded sharp
  Cheddar cheese

¼ cup grated Parmesan cheese
4 medium tomatoes, peeled
  and sliced
½ cup dry bread or corn flake
  crumbs
2 tablespoons butter or
  margarine, melted

Heat oil in skillet. Cook garlic for a few minutes, then discard. Saute zucchini in the oil until lightly browned. Combine seasoned salt and cheeses. Make alternate layers in casserole of zucchini and tomatoes, sprinkling each with cheese. Toss crumbs and butter and spread over top. Bake in 350° oven for 20 to 25 minutes. Makes 6 servings.

BARLEY PILAF

½ cup butter or margarine
1 large onion, chopped
2 cups pearl barley
5 cups (approximately) hot
   chicken broth

1½ teaspoons salt
½ teaspoon fresh ground pepper
½ cup finely chopped green
   onions
¼ cup finely chopped parsley
1 cup lightly salted, toasted
   cashews

Heat butter in heavy skillet. Add onion and cook until soft and golden. Add barley and stir over low heat till coated with butter and lightly tan. Transfer to 2 quart buttered casserole and add ⅔ of the boiling chicken broth, or enough to cover barley generously. Season. Cover dish tightly and bake in 350° oven 25 to 30 minutes. Stir in green onions, parsley and remaining broth. Cook 15 minutes longer or till broth is absorbed and grains puffed and tender. Adjust seasoning. Keep warm in slow oven till ready to serve. Toss in whole cashews before serving. Makes 12 servings.

GARLIC GRITS

4 cups boiling water
1 teaspoon salt
1 cup grits

½ cup butter
½ pound processed cheese, cubed
3 eggs, beaten
½ teaspoon garlic salt

Cook grits in salted, boiling water until thick. Add remaining ingredients. Mix well. Place in buttered, 1½-quart casserole. Bake in 350° oven for 45 minutes. Makes 6 servings.

BUFFET POTATO CASSEROLE

Tastes like the stuffing for twice-baked potatoes. But so much easier!

1 2-pound package frozen hash brown potatoes	½ cup chopped onion
½ cup butter or margarine, melted	2 cups shredded cheddar cheese
1 pint dairy sour cream	1 teaspoon salt
1 can condensed cream of chicken soup	½ teaspoon pepper
	2 cups corn flake crumbs
	½ cup butter or margarine, melted

Combine potatoes and ½ cup melted butter in large bowl. Stir in sour cream, soup, onion, cheese, salt and pepper. Place in greased 13x9x2-inch baking dish. Combine corn flake crumbs and ½ cup melted butter. Sprinkle over top.

Cover with foil. Bake in 350° oven 20 minutes. Uncover and continue baking 20 minutes. Makes 12 servings.

Note: The casserole can be made in advance and refrigerated. If so, add 10 minutes to baking time.

CREAMY SCALLOPED POTATOES

A smooth and rich potato casserole with the added flavor of mushrooms.

2 pounds potatoes (about 6 medium)	1 10½-ounce can condensed cream of mushroom soup
1 small onion, thinly sliced	1 cup milk
¼ cup flour	1 4-ounce can sliced mushrooms, drained
1 teaspoon salt	
½ teaspoon pepper	4 slices process American cheese
3 tablespoons butter or margarine	

Wash and thinly slice unpeeled potatoes. Drain. Put half of sliced potatoes in greased 2-quart casserole. Top with half of onion slices, flour, salt and pepper. Add remaining sliced potatoes and onions. Sprinkle with remaining flour. Add butter (in bits), mushroom soup and milk. Cover and bake in 350° oven 45 minutes. Remove from oven and add mushrooms; stir. Return to oven for 30 minutes, covered. Top with cheese slices and bake 15 more minutes uncovered. Makes 8 servings.

FOIL-WRAPPED POTATOES

These cook on the grill, along with your meat.

3 large baking potatoes or 6 smaller	1 large onion, sliced
Salt and pepper	½ pound sharp process American cheese, cubed
4 or 5 slices bacon, crisp-cooked	½ cup butter or margarine

Slice unpeeled potatoes onto 6 large pieces of foil. Sprinkle with salt and pepper. Crumble bacon over. Add onion rings and cheese cubes. Slice butter over all. Bring edges up and, leaving a little space for expansion of steam, seal well with double fold.

Place packages on grill. Cook over coals about 1 hour or till done (about 45 minutes for covered grill). Makes 6 servings.

GRILLED DEVILED POTATOES

Good accompaniment with almost any meat and especially good with Gingered Ham Slice.

3 cups mashed potatoes	½ teaspoon sugar
½ cup sour cream	2 tablespoons chopped green onion
1 teaspoon prepared mustard	
½ teaspoon salt	Paprika

Mix all ingredients together except paprika. Spoon into 4 baking shells made from heavy duty aluminum foil. Spinkle tops with paprika. Place on grill or in oven for 25 to 30 minutes or until heated through. May be made ahead and refrigerated. If so, add 10 minutes to cooking time. Makes 4 servings.

JALAPENO POTATOES

4 medium potatoes	¼ cup butter or margarine
1 small bell pepper, chopped	1 tablespoon flour
1 2-ounce jar pimientos,	1 cup milk
drained and chopped	½ roll jalapeno cheese, cubed
1 teaspoon salt	½ roll garlic cheese, cubed
½ teaspoon pepper	

Boil potatoes in jackets in salted water until tender, but not falling apart. When cool, peel, slice and layer in 1½-quart buttered casserole with bell pepper and pimiento. Salt and pepper each layer. Melt butter in saucepan, add flour and stir until well blended. Gradually add milk, stirring constantly. Add cheese and cook and stir until melted. Pour over potatoes and bake in 350° oven 1 hour. Makes 4 servings.

POTATOES HASHED IN CREAM

A delicious, rich-tasting way to serve potatoes.

6 medium potatoes, boiled and cubed	2 teaspoons salt
4 tablespoons butter, margarine or bacon drippings	Freshly ground pepper
1 tablespoon flour	½ cup light cream
	Paprika

Cut boiled potatoes into cubes and saute them in butter, margarine, or bacon drippings until they are heated through. Sprinkle with flour, salt and pepper. Gradually pour in cream to cover bottom of pan and let potatoes cook in the cream. Be careful not to let them scorch. Sprinkle liberally with paprika. For different taste treat, sprinkle liberally with grated parmesan cheese. Serves 6 to 8.

RICE FIESTA

Spicy treatment for rice.

1 cup chopped onions	1 teaspoon chili powder
1 tablespoon oil	2 cups beef broth
1 cup uncooked rice, long grain	1 16-ounce can chili without beans
1 teaspoon salt	2 cups grated Cheddar cheese

Saute onions in oil until tender but not brown. Add rice, seasonings and broth. Bring to a boil. Stir well; cover, reduce heat and simmer 15 minutes or until rice is tender and liquid absorbed. Stir in chili. Spoon half the mixture into greased shallow 1½ quart casserole. Sprinkle with 1 cup cheese. Add remaining rice mixture and top with cheese. Bake in 350° oven for 15 to 20 minutes or until bubbly. Makes 6 servings.

RICE PILAF

Rich tasting, easy to make and so good.

4 tablespoons butter or margarine	¼ teaspoon tabasco sauce
1 cup diced celery	1 8-ounce can peas
½ cup chopped almonds	1 4-ounce can sliced mushrooms
2 tablespoons chopped onion	8 ripe olives, chopped
2 chicken bouillon cubes	2 tablespoons raisins
½ teaspoon salt	2 cups raw pre-cooked rice

Melt butter in a large skillet; add celery, almonds, and onion. Cook over low heat for 5 minutes. Add bouillon cubes, salt and tabasco. Drain the liquid from the peas and mushrooms and add water to make 2½ cups. Add this to the skillet along with the peas, mushrooms, olives and raisins. Bring to a boil. Add the rice and toss with fork to moisten. Cover and remove from heat, Let stand 5 minutes. Makes 4 to 6 servings.

WILD RICE CASSEROLE

Delicious! Nothing else to say!

1 cup wild rice
1 10½-ounce can consomme
¾ cup chopped celery
¼ cup chopped onion

1 3-ounce can sliced
  mushrooms, drained
4 tablespoons butter or
  margarine, melted
½ teaspoon salt
1/8 teaspoon pepper

Wash rice in several waters. Place in buttered 1½-quart casserole and add remaining ingredients. Let stand for 3 hours or overnight. Bake, covered, in 350° oven for 2 hours or until rice is tender. Stir once during cooking. Makes 6 servings.

CURRIED FRUIT

Good with Iowa Ham Balls.

⅓ cup butter or margarine
¾ cup brown sugar, packed
1 or 2 teaspoons curry powder
1 16-ounce can pear halves

1 20-ounce can pineapple chunks
1 16-ounce can peach or apricot
  halves
12 maraschino cherries

Melt butter, add sugar and curry. Drain fruit well and dry. Make attractive arrangement in 2-quart casserole, placing maraschino cherries in center of peach and pear halves. Spoon butter mixture over top. Bake in 350° oven 1 hour. Serve warm. Makes 10 servings.

HOT FRUIT COMPOTE

Serve this as an accompaniment to meat, especially pork.

12   almond or coconut
     macaroons, crumbled
4   cups canned fruits, drained
     (apricots, pitted cherries,
     peaches, pears, pineapple,
     mandarin oranges, etc.)

½   cup slivered almonds, toasted
¼   cup sherry
¼   cup brown sugar, packed
¼   cup melted butter

Cover bottom of a 2 quart casserole with cookie crumbs. Alternate
fruit and cookie crumbs, finishing with crumbs. Sprinkle over top:
almonds, sherry and sugar. Bake in 350° oven 30 minutes. Remove
from oven, pour melted butter over top. Serve hot. Makes 8 servings.

FRUIT BASKET SALAD

*The clear, lemony dressing for this salad adds delicious flavor and
also keeps the fruit from turning brown. Can be made several hours
in advance and is good for carrying in the cooler to picnics.*

1   fresh pineapple, cut up (with
    juice) or 1   20-ounce can
    pineapple chunks (with
    juice)
2   oranges, peeled and
    sectioned

½   cup sugar
6   cups cut-up fresh fruit
    (strawberries, melon, peaches,
    grapes, bananas)
2   tablespoons cornstarch
    Juice of 1 lemon

The night before, combine pineapple, juice, oranges and sugar.
Cover and let stand in refrigerator overnight.

Drain off juice and add water to make 1 cup. Blend liquid into
cornstarch; add lemon juice. Heat to boiling. When cool, mix with
orange-pineapple mixture and remaining fruit. Cover til serving time.
Makes 8 servings.

For a winter salad, fix pineapple and oranges as above and
substitute apples and bananas for summer fruit.

BUFFET SALAD

This multi-ingredient salad makes great party fare. Should be made a day or more in advance as flavor improves with age.

1	head cauliflower, separated	2	6-ounce cans pitted ripe olives
1	16-ounce can green beans, drained	2	5-ounce cans pimento stuffed olives
1	16-ounce can wax beans, drained	1	14-ounce can artichokes, quartered
1	bunch celery, sliced	1	2-ounce carton frozen chives
1	pound carrots, sliced	2	15-ounce cans kidney beans, drained
1	pint cherry tomatoes		
2	13-ounce jars yellow pickle corn relish	2	16-ounce cans garbanzo beans, drained
2	4-ounce cans button mushrooms, drained	2	8-ounce bottles creamy onion dressing
		1	16-ounce bottle Italian dressing

Mix all ingredients together. Serves 24.

GREEK SALAD

Feta cheese makes the difference!

1	small head of lettuce, shredded	2	tomatoes, cut in thin wedges
1	small cucumber, thinly sliced	12	Greek olives
		⅓	cup olive oil
1	small bunch radishes, thinly sliced	¼	cup wine vinegar
		1	teaspoon dried oregano
3	green onions, cut in short pieces	1	teaspoon salt
			Feta cheese
			Anchovy fillets, optional

Combine lettuce, cucumber, radishes, onions, tomatoes and olives in salad bowl. In jar combine olive oil, vinegar, oregano and salt. Shake well. Pour over salad; toss. Serve in individual salad bowls. Top each with a slice of cheese and 2 anchovy filets, if desired. Makes 4 servings. (Feta cheese and Greek olives available in specialty food stores).

GUACAMOLE SALAD

1	pint cherry tomatoes	¼	cup salad oil
1	green pepper, chopped	2	tablespoons lemon juice
1	small onion, sliced and	½	teaspoon garlic salt
	separated into rings	6	cups torn lettuce
½	cup chopped celery	1	6-ounce package frozen
½	cup pitted ripe olives		guacamole dip, thawed

Combine tomatoes, green pepper, onion, celery and olives. Mix oil, lemon juice and garlic salt and pour over combined vegetables. Chill 30 minutes (or longer). Add to lettuce and toss. Divide among 6 individual salad bowls. Spoon guacamole dip over each. Makes 6 servings.

ROQUEFORT SALAD

2	cloves garlic		Freshly ground pepper
6	tablespoons salad oil		Salt
2	cups crisp croutons	¼	cup grated Parmesan cheese
3	quarts crisp, chilled salad	½	cup crumbled Roquefort
	greens		cheese
1	tablespoon Worchestershire	1	uncooked egg, unbeaten
	sauce	½	cup lemon juice

Allow garlic cloves to stand in the oil for several hours. Remove and discard garlic. Stir croutons in oil and remove. Put aside to add to salad. Place salad greens in bowl. Add next five ingredients. Break raw egg onto salad, pour on lemon juice and toss salad thoroughly until each leaf is coated. Add the croutons and serve immediately. Makes 8 servings.

SAN FRANCISCO SALAD

2 14-ounce cans artichoke hearts, chopped

1 14-ounce can heart of palm, chopped

1 6-ounce can pitted black olives, chopped

1 8-ounce bottle San Francisco dressing

1 head lettuce

Mix all ingredients except lettuce and marinate overnight or several hours. Break lettuce in bite size pieces and pour marinated vegetables over. Serve at once. Makes 6 to 8 servings.

BLUE CHEESE SALAD GLEN

Try broiling your salad for a change.

2 firm heads lettuce

¾ cup blue cheese or Roquefort dressing

¾ cup crumbled blue cheese

6 slices bacon, cooked crisp and crumbled

Cut one-inch slices from firm head lettuce. This will make 6 good slices. Place on ungreased baking sheet. Spread 2 tablespoons of dressing on each slice, then sprinkle with the cheese. Pre-heat oven broiler. Broil the lettuce for about 60 seconds about 3 inches from heat. Sprinkle with bacon and serve. Makes 6 servings.

In July, 1929, the first dial telephone in Des Moines was installed at Terrace Hill.

FRESH SPINACH SALAD AND DRESSING

2 pounds fresh spinach	3 hard-cooked eggs, chopped
1 can drained bean sprouts	½ pound cooked, crumbled
1 cup chopped water chestnuts	bacon

Wash and dry fresh spinach and tear into serving size pieces. Combine with remaining ingredients. Pour dressing over, toss and serve. Makes 6 to 8 servings.

Dressing: Mix 1 cup oil, ⅓ cup catsup, 1 tablespoon Worchestershire sauce, ¾ cup sugar, ¼ cup vinegar and 2 tablespoons minced onion in a blender.

SPINACH SALAD

¼ cup sugar	⅓ cup vinegar
1 teaspoon salt	1 small onion, minced
1 teaspoon pepper	1 clove garlic, minced
1 teaspoon dry mustard	1½ pounds fresh spinach
½ teaspoon celery salt	½ pound bacon, crisp-cooked
1 cup oil	and crumbled
½ cup catsup	6 hard-cooked eggs, sliced

Combine sugar, salt, pepper, dry mustard, celery salt, oil, catsup, vinegar, minced onion and garlic. Shake well to mix. Chill 24 hours.

Combine spinach, bacon and hard-cooked eggs in salad bowl. Pour on enough dressing to coat leaves and toss gently. Makes 6 servings.

FRESH MUSHROOM SALAD

1 large head romaine	Freshly ground black pepper
½ pound raw mushrooms, sliced	¾ cup walnuts, chopped (optional)
4 to 6 scallions, chopped	French Dressing

Break romaine into salad bowl. Add mushrooms, scallions, pepper and walnuts. Toss with French Dressing and serve. Makes 4 to 6 servings.

French Dressing: ½ cup salad oil, 2 tablespoons vinegar, 2 tablespoons lemon juice, ½ teaspoon salt, ¼ teaspoon dry mustard and ¼ teaspoon paprika. Beat all ingredients together well. Keep in covered container in refrigerator. Before serving, shake to blend. Makes ¾ cup.

MIXED VEGETABLE SALAD

2 large (20-ounce) packages   2 teaspoons vinegar
   frozen mixed vegetables,   1 teaspoon dill seed
   cooked, drained and chilled ½ teaspoon sugar
2 tablespoons chopped parsley ½ cup mayonnaise
2 green onions, chopped   1 can asparagus tips, drained,
¼ teaspoon seasoned salt   optional

For dressing, combine all ingredients except asparagus. Gently blend mixed vegetables with dressing. Let stand in refrigerator at least one hour. Heap into bowls lined with salad greens. Arrange asparagus tips on top as a garnish if desired. Serves 12.

ZUCCHINI AND RICE SALAD

2   pounds zucchini   2   cups hot cooked rice
2   tablespoons salt   ½   cup thinly sliced green onions
¼   cup lemon juice   ½   cup pitted ripe olives
1   tablespoon salt   ½   cup sliced radishes
¼   teaspoon pepper   ½   cup chopped pimiento
⅔   to 1 cup salad oil

Halve zucchini lengthwise and thinly slice. Place in colander. Sprinkle with 2 tablespoons salt, toss and let drain 30 minutes. Press out moisture and pat dry with paper toweling.

In large bowl, combine lemon juice, 1 tablespoon salt and pepper. Add the oil in a stream, beating until it is well combined. Stir in rice and zucchini and toss. Add remaining ingredients. Chill at least 2 hours. Serve on a platter lined with lettuce leaves. Makes 8 to 10 servings.

From the reminiscences of butler Elmer Nelson's daughter: "The garage was used for the cars on the main floor and below when Dad was first there they had a family cow in the stable, and on the steeple they raised pigeons, as Mr. F. M. Hubbell was (mainly) a vegetarian and only ate squab which (was) raised for him."

SALAD DRESSING de la MAISON

This classic dressing has a special tanginess and is good on all green salads.

¼ cup red wine vinegar
½ teaspoon salt
Freshly ground pepper

2 to 4 teaspoons Dijon-style mustard
½ cup vegetable oil
¼ cup olive oil

In small bowl, combine vinegar, salt, pepper and mustard. Add oil slowly, whisking constantly. (Or combine vinegar, salt, mustard and pepper in food processor bowl with blade inserted. With motor running, slowly add oil through food tube.) Store in cruet; shake before using. Note: If you prefer the flavor of olive oil to predominate, use ½ cup olive oil and ¼ cup vegetable oil. Makes 1 cup.

MAYTAG BLUE CHEESE DRESSING #1

2 ounces Maytag blue cheese
½ cup mayonnaise
3 tablespoons light cream
1 teaspoon sugar
1 teaspoon dried parsley flakes
2 teaspoons lemon juice

2 teaspoons vinegar
1 teaspoon grated onion
½ teaspoon Worcestershire sauce
½ teaspoon prepared horseradish
¼ teaspoon garlic salt
Dash fresh ground pepper

Have cheese at room temperature. Add mayonnaise; blend thoroughly until smooth. Add remaining ingredients; mix well. Cover and chill. Makes about 1 cup.

MAYTAG BLUE CHEESE DRESSING #2

4 ounces Maytag blue cheese
1 cup mayonnaise
½ cup dairy sour cream
½ to 1 clove garlic, minced

2 tablespoons finely cut green onions and tops
1 tablespoon wine vinegar
1 tablespoon lemon juice
1 teaspoon sugar

Combine all ingredients. Cover and chill. Makes about 2 cups.

DESSERTS

FROZEN ORANGE SOUFFLE GRAND MARNIER

Delightfully easy, elegant frozen dessert.

6　egg yolks	8　cleaned orange shells,
¾　cup sugar	souffle cups, or sherbet
2　cups heavy cream, whipped	dishes
2　to 3 ounces Grand Marnier	Powdered cocoa (optional)

Combine egg yolks and sugar; beat until thick and lemon colored. Fold 2 cups of the whipped cream into the yolk-sugar mixture. Fold in the Grand Marnier. Fill the cups with the mixture and place in the freezer for at least 2 hours. At serving time, sift cocoa over souffles, if desired.

CHOCOLATE MINT FRANGOS

These have a lovely velvety texture. Also, they are ready to serve directly from the freezer. Remove papers and place frangos in sherbet dishes or on individual plates.

1　cup slightly softened butter	4　eggs
2　cups sifted confectioners'	2　teaspoons peppermint flavoring
sugar	2　teaspoons vanilla
4　squares semi-sweet	¼　cup chopped nuts, if desired
chocolate	

Beat butter and sugar until light and fluffy. Melt chocolate and cool slightly. Add to butter mixture. Beat eggs and add to chocolate mixture. Beat until light and fluffy. Add flavorings and beat well. Spoon into paper cupcake liners. Sprinkle with chopped nuts, if desired. Freeze. Store in freezer. Makes 18.

CHOCOLATE ANGEL MOUSSE

This dessert brings raves!

1 pint (2 cups) whipping cream	4 cups torn angel food cake
½ cup sugar	(half a 10-inch cake or 1
1 teaspoon vanilla	small cake)
3 eggs, separated	1 12-ounce package chocolate
2 tablespoons sugar	chips

Whip cream with ½ cup sugar and vanilla. Beat egg yolks and egg whites separately. Butter a 9x5x3-inch loaf pan. Layer half of cake bits in bottom of pan. Melt chocolate chips in a double boiler or microwave oven. Allow to cool 10 minutes. Add 2 tablespoons sugar and egg yolks. Fold in egg whites and whipped cream mixture. Pour half of mixture over cake bits. Layer remainder of cake bits in pan and pour remaining mixture on top. Refrigerate several hours before serving. Makes 8 servings.

STRAWBERRY SUBLIME

This easy, frozen dessert truly lives up to its name.

1 cup all purpose flour	2 egg whites
¼ cup brown sugar, packed	1 10-ounce package frozen
½ cup butter or margarine	strawberries, partially thawed
½ cup chopped walnuts	1 cup heavy cream, whipped
1 cup sugar	½ teaspoon vanilla
2 tablespoons lemon juice	

Mix the flour, brown sugar, butter and walnuts together. Spread out on cookie sheet with sides and bake in 375° oven for 10 minutes or until brown.

Combine and beat the sugar, lemon juice, egg white and strawberries at high speed in blender for 15 minutes. Fold in whipped cream and vanilla. Place ½ baked crumbs on bottom of 13x9x2-inch pan or 2 8-inch pie plates. Pour filling in pan and sprinkle remaining crumbs on top. Freeze at least 6 hours. Makes 10 to 12 servings.

CHEESE BLINTZES IN CARAMEL SAUCE

A chafing dish dessert good for serving buffet style.

⅔ cup all-purpose flour
2 tablespoons sugar
Dash salt
2 eggs
1¼ cups milk
2 tablespoons butter

1 12-ounce carton or 1½ cups
   cream-style cottage cheese,
   drained
¼ cup sour cream
2 tablespoons sugar
¼ teaspoon salt
½ teaspoon vanilla
1 recipe Caramel Sauce

Stir together flour, sugar, salt, eggs, milk and butter in a bowl. Beat until smooth with rotary beater. Heat a 6-inch skillet until a drop of water will "dance" on surface. Grease lightly and pour in 2 tablespoons batter. Lift skillet off heat and tilt from side to side until batter covers bottom evenly. Return skillet to heat and cook until underside is lightly browned, about 1½ minutes. To remove, invert skillet over paper toweling. Repeat with remaining batter. Makes 18 crepes.

Combine cottage cheese, sour cream, sugar, salt and vanilla. Spoon 1 tablespoon of mixture on unbrowned side of crepe. Roll crepe by folding two opposite sides of crepe over each other. Fold ends into center. Place seam side down in chafing dish. (If making in advance, place in pan, cover and refrigerate several hours or overnight.)

Pour hot Caramel Sauce over blintzes in chafing dish. Simmer, covered, 10 or 15 minutes, until heated through.

Caramel Sauce: Melt 3 tablespoons butter in small sauce pan. Add 1 cup brown sugar, packed, a dash of salt and ¼ cup water. Cook and stir over low heat until mixture comes to a boil. Remove from heat and stir in ¼ cup orange-flavored liqueur.

Despite the numerous parties and dining occasions, F. M. Hubbell regarded overeating as one of man's most deadly foes. He credited his good health to a light diet.

The recipes on this page were saved by Blenda Friedmeyer, head housekeeper for the Hubbell Family at Terrace Hill for over 40 years, until the house was closed.

CREME BRULEE

Often served by Anna Hubbell when she entertained ladies at luncheon.

8 egg yolks	5 tablespoons granulated sugar
1 pint light cream	2 teaspoons vanilla
	2 tablespoons brown sugar

Beat egg yolks. Scald cream. Remove cream from heat and pour very slowly into egg mixture, stirring constantly. Add granulated sugar and vanilla. Pour mixture into 1½-quart baking dish and place in pan of hot water. Bake in 350° oven about 1 hour, or until silver knife inserted in center comes out clean.

Remove from oven, sprinkle with brown sugar. Place custard in pan of crushed ice. Place under broiler until sugar melts and forms a glaze. Serve cold. Makes 8 servings.

COFFEE JELLO

This was such a favorite of Grover Hubbell's, it was served to him at lunch every day!

1 envelope unflavored gelatin	1 cup strong coffee
⅓ cup sugar	1 teaspoon vanilla
1 cup boiling water	Heavy cream, plain or whipped

Combine gelatin and sugar. Add boiling water and stir until sugar is dissolved. Add coffee and vanilla and stir to mix. Chill until set. Serve in individual dessert dishes and top with plain or whipped cream.

Grover Hubbell's granddaughter Anne Weaver remembered Christmas celebrations at Terrace Hill complete with roast suckling pig or a feast of roast goose raised on the grounds.

In the summer Mah-jong was played on the screened porch. Croquet was played on the back lawn.

Mrs. Weaver was married at Terrace Hill herself, in 1952.

TWO-TONED CHEESE CAKE

1¼ cups graham cracker crumbs	½ cup sugar
¼ cup butter, melted	3 medium eggs
¼ cup sugar	¾ teaspoon vanilla
1 pound cream cheese, softened	1 pint sour cream
	¼ cup sugar
	1 teaspoon vanilla

Mix crumbs, melted butter and sugar. Cover bottom of a 9-inch spring form pan. Beat cream cheese until light and fluffy. Beat in ½ cup sugar, eggs and ¾ teaspoon vanilla. Pour over crust. Bake in 375° oven 20 minutes. Remove from oven and cool 15 minutes. Prepare topping with wooden spoon, blending sour cream, ¼ cup sugar and 1 teaspoon vanilla. Spoon gently over top. Bake in 475° oven for 10 minutes. Remove and let stand at room temperature 2 to 4 hours. Chill at least 12 hours before serving. Makes 10 to 12 servings.

INDIVIDUAL CHEESE CAKES

½ cup graham cracker crumbs	3 egg yolks
2 8-ounce packages cream cheese, softened	3 egg whites, stiffly beaten
¾ cup sugar	¾ cup sour cream
	2½ teaspoons sugar
	1 teaspoon vanilla

Butter tiny muffin tins and sprinkle with crumbs. Mix and beat until smooth cream cheese, sugar and egg yolks. Fold in beaten egg whites. Fill pans almost full. Bake in 350° oven 15 minutes. Cool in pan 15 minutes. (Cakes will puff up while baking, then sink while cooling.) Combine sour cream, sugar and vanilla and fill center of dropped cakes. Bake in 400° oven 5 minutes. Top with cherry or strawberry slice, a blueberry or a piece of glaceed fruit. Store in refrigerator. May be frozen if desired. Thaw before serving. Makes 48.

CHOCOLATE SHEET CAKE

Melt-in-your-mouth, milk chocolate cake the children will love.

2 cups sifted all-purpose flour	1 tablespoon cocoa
2 cups sugar	1 cup water
1 teaspoon baking soda	½ cup buttermilk
¼ teaspoon salt	2 beaten eggs
1 cup butter	1 teaspoon vanilla

Sift together dry ingredients. Melt butter; stir in cocoa and water. Pour over dry ingredients and mix well. Stir in buttermilk, eggs and vanilla.

Pour into greased 15x10x1-inch pan. Bake in 375° oven 17 to 20 minutes. Spread with Chocolate Frosting while cake is hot. Makes 20 servings.

Chocolate Frosting: Place ½ cup butter and 6 tablespoons milk in saucepan. Bring to a boil. Stir in 3 tablespoons cocoa, 1 pound confectioners' sugar and 1 teaspoon vanilla.

ITALIAN CREAM CAKE

5 eggs, separated	2 cups all-purpose flour
2 cups sugar	1 teaspoon baking soda
½ cup butter, softened	¾ teaspoon salt
½ cup shortening	1 cup coconut, shredded
1 teaspoon vanilla	1 cup buttermilk

Beat egg whites and set aside. Cream sugar, butter, shortening and vanilla. Add egg yolks, one at a time. Stir together dry ingredients, including coconut. Add to creamed mixture alternately with buttermilk. Pour into 3 greased and floured 8 or 9-inch round cake pans. Bake in 350° oven 30 minutes. Frost with Cream Cheese Pecan Frosting.

Cream Cheese Pecan Frosting: Cream ½ cup softened butter, 8 ounces softened cream cheese and 1 teaspoon vanilla. Beat in 1 1-pound box confectioners' sugar. Add 1 cup chopped pecans, optional.

SAVARIN CHANTILLY

Spectacular, apricot glazed, feather light yeast cake for that special occasion.

1 package active dry yeast	½ teaspoon salt
¼ cup warm water	2 cups sifted all-purpose flour
½ cup milk, scalded	1 egg
⅓ cup butter or margarine, softened	Savarin Syrup
	Apricot Glaze
¼ cup sugar	Creme Chantilly

Soften active dry yeast in warm water. To hot milk, add butter, sugar and salt; stir until butter melts. Cool to lukewarm.

Stir in ½ cup of the flour. Beat in egg and yeast mixture. Add remaining flour. Beat dough vigorously 5 to 7 minutes.

Cover and let rise in warm place until double, about 1¼ hours. Stir down batter and spoon into well-greased 6-cup ring mold. Cover; let rise until almost double, about 45 minutes.

Bake in 350° oven 35 minutes or until lightly browned. Cool 5 minutes and remove from mold. Prick top of Savarin with toothpick and drizzle with Savarin Syrup. Let stand about 30 minutes, basting frequently to soak well. Brush entire surface with warm Apricot Glaze. Trim top with blanched almonds and candied cherries. At serving time, fill center with Creme Chantilly. Makes 14 servings.

Savarin Syrup: Combine 1 cup sugar and 2 cups water; bring to boil. Remove from heat and cool to lukewarm. Stir in ½ cup kirsch, rum or cognac.

Apricot Glaze: Heat and stir one 12-ounce jar apricot preserves.

Creme Chantilly: Whip 2 cups heavy cream with 2 tablespoons confectioners' sugar and 2 teaspoons vanilla.

Weddings and anniversaries have always played an important part in the scene at Terrace Hill. Grover Hubbell's daughter Helen Virginia was married there twice. Other daughters Frances and Mary Belle had lavish receptions there after their wedding ceremonies. In 1955, Anna and Grover Hubbell celebrated their fiftieth wedding anniversary in the mansion with 300 guests.

CHOCOLATE POUND CAKE

A rich, moist cake, excellent for picnics and lunch boxes.

1 cup butter or margarine	3 cups all-purpose flour
½ cup shortening	½ teaspoon baking powder
3 cups sugar	½ teaspoon salt
5 eggs	4 tablespoons cocoa
1 teaspoon vanilla	1 cup milk

Cream together butter and shortening. Add sugar and mix well. Add eggs, one at a time, beating after each addition. Add vanilla. Combine dry ingredients and add alternately with milk to creamed mixture. Bake in greased and floured 10-inch tube pan at 325° for 80 minutes. Makes 14 to 16 servings.

RUM CAKE

½ cup chopped pecans	¾ cup water
1 package butter pecan cake mix	¾ cup light rum
4 eggs	1 package (3-ounce) instant vanilla pudding mix
½ cup oil	1 recipe Glaze

Grease and flour bundt or angel food cake pan. Put nuts in bottom of pan. Beat together cake mix, eggs, oil, ½ cup water, ½ cup rum and pudding mix. Pour in pan and bake in 325° oven 40 minutes. While cake is baking, make glaze. Pour over cake while both are hot. Leave in pan for a day or two before serving. Unmold.

Glaze: Boil for 10 minutes ½ cup butter, 1 cup sugar ¼ cup rum and ¼ cup water.

CARAMEL FROSTING

1 cup brown sugar, packed	½ cup butter or margarine
¼ cup milk	3 cups sifted confectioners' sugar

Combine first 3 ingredients in saucepan. Bring to boil, stirring constantly. Cook 10 minutes. Gradually add confectioners' sugar until well blended. If desired, add ½ cup pecans. Use on white or chocolate cake.

EASY ZUPPA INGLESE

The translation for this famous Italian dessert is "English Soup," a take-off on the traditional English Trifle.

1 package (1 pound 2 ounce) yellow cake mix	1 recipe Rum Custard
	2 cups heavy cream, whipped
1 teaspoon orange peel, grated	Slivered, toasted almonds or
1 recipe Orange Rum Syrup	chocolate curls, optional

Prepare cake mix as directed on package, adding orange peel. Grease and flour a 9 or 10-inch springform pan. Pour in cake batter and bake at 350° until toothpick inserted into center comes out clean—40 to 45 minutes. Cool completely on rack.

Remove pan side from cake, leaving cake on base. Carefully cut cake horizontally into 3 layers. Lift off top two layers. Replace pan sides around bottom holding the remaining cake layer.

Drizzle bottom layer with one-third of Orange Rum Syrup; spread with one-third of custard. Repeat with next layer. On top layer, prick top of cake all over with toothpick. Sprinkle with remaining syrup and top with remaining custard. Chill at least 6 hours or overnight.

Before serving, remove pan sides. Spread top and sides with 1 cup whipped cream. Garnish with almonds or chocolate curls, if desired. Serves 12.

Orange Rum Syrup: Combine 6 tablespoons sugar, 6 tablespoons water and 1 teaspoon grated orange peel. Bring to boil and boil 3 minutes. Remove from heat and cool. Add 5 tablespoons light rum.

Rum Custard: Blend 1 package (4½-ounce) custard mix and 2½ cups milk. Bring to a boil, stirring constantly. Add 4 tablespoons light rum. Place pan in bowl of ice water. Cool, stirring constantly to keep custard from setting up. Fold 1 cup heavy cream, whipped, into custard.

Variation for chocolate lovers: Divide Rum Custard in half and spread on bottom two layers. Reduce whipped cream for outside of cake to ½ cup. Frost top of cake with chocolate butter frosting (whip with a fork 2 tablespoons soft butter; 1 square unsweetened chocolate, melted; 1½ cups powdered sugar; ½ teaspoon vanilla). Cover sides with whipped cream.

GLAZED ORANGE CAKE

A moist and luscious fresh orange cake worth the time it takes.

3 cups cake flour	½ teaspoon vanilla
1 tablespoon baking powder	2 tablespoons grated orange
1/8 teaspoon salt	rind
1 cup butter	5 eggs
2 cups sugar	¾ cup milk

Sift the cake flour, baking powder, and salt together twice. Cream the butter and sugar until light and fluffy. Add vanilla and orange rind. Add eggs one at a time, beating well after each addition. Add the flour mixture alternately with the milk, ending with the flour. Mix well after each addition. Spoon into a floured, buttered 10-inch tube pan and bake in a 350° oven for about 1 hour, until cake springs back to the touch. Cool in pan on rack for only 2 minutes and glaze immediately.

Orange Glaze: Heat ¼ cup butter, ⅔ cup sugar and ⅓ cup orange juice in a saucepan until the sugar is dissolved. Make the glaze so that it is ready when the cake is baked. Pour evenly over cake in pan while cake is still hot. Allow cake to cool thoroughly before removing from pan. Makes 14 to 16 servings.

Pumpkin Pecan Pie

4 slightly beaten eggs	½ teaspoon cinnamon
2 cups canned or mashed cooked pumpkin	¼ teaspoon salt
1 cup sugar	1 unbaked 9-inch pie shell
½ cup dark corn syrup	1 cup chopped pecans
1 teaspoon vanilla	

Combine ingredients except pecans. Pour into pie shell—top with pecans. Bake at 350 degrees for 40 minutes, or until set.

With best wishes, *Nancy Reagan*

New Year's Eve at Terrace Hill Usually meant a party, with a group photograph taken on the staircase. This one was taken in the early 1950's. The participants are identified on the next page.

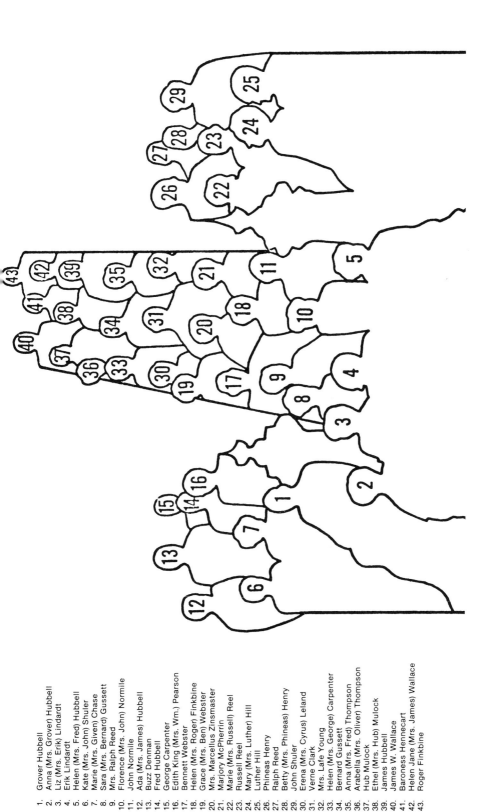

1. Grover Hubbell
2. Anna (Mrs. Grover) Hubbell
3. Liz (Mrs. Erik) Lindardt
4. Erik Lindardt
5. Helen (Mrs. Fred) Hubbell
6. Kate (Mrs. John) Shuler
7. Marie (Mrs. Given) Chase
8. Sara (Mrs. Bernard) Gussett
9. Mrs. Ralph Reed
10. Florence (Mrs. John) Normile
11. John Normile
12. Ada (Mrs. James) Hubbell
13. Buzz Denman
14. Fred Hubbell
15. George Carpenter
16. Edith King (Mrs. Wm.) Pearson
17. Bennett Webster
18. Helen (Mrs. Roger) Finkbine
19. Grace (Mrs. Ben) Webster
20. Mrs. Marcellus Zinsmaster
21. Marjory McPherrin
22. Marie (Mrs. Russell) Reel
23. Russell Reel
24. Mary (Mrs. Luther) Hill
25. Luther Hill
26. Phineas Henry
27. Ralph Reed
28. Betty (Mrs. Phineas) Henry
29. John Shuler
30. Erena (Mrs. Cyrus) Leland
31. Verne Clark
32. Mrs. Lafe Young
33. Helen (Mrs. George) Carpenter
34. Bernard Gussett
35. Anna (Mrs. Fred) Thompson
36. Arabella (Mrs. Oliver) Thompson
37. Hub Mulock
38. Ethel (Mrs. Hub) Mulock
39. James Hubbell
40. James W. Wallace
41. Baroness Hennecart
42. Helen Jane (Mrs. James) Wallace
43. Roger Finkbine

PEACH MELBA ICE CREAM PIE

This is a cool version of the famous peach-raspberry combination named for Australian soprano Nellie Melba.

1 3½-ounce can flaked coconut	1 pint vanilla ice cream, softened
½ cup finely chopped walnuts	1 10-ounce package frozen red raspberries, thawed
2 tablespoons melted butter	
1 quart peach ice cream, softened	½ cup sugar
	1 tablespoon cornstarch
	2 cups sliced peaches, sweetened

Combine coconut, nuts and butter. Press firmly and evenly against bottom and sides of a 9-inch pie plate. Bake in 325° oven 10 to 15 minutes or until golden brown. Cool.

Spoon peach ice cream into crust, spreading to edges. Freeze until firm. Spoon vanilla ice cream over peach. Freeze. Drain raspberries, reserving syrup. Add sugar and cornstarch to syrup and cook over medium heat, stirring constantly, until thickened. Boil 2 minutes longer. Stir in raspberries; cool. Just before serving, arrange peaches on pie. Cut into wedges. Serve with raspberry sauce. Makes 6 to 8 servings.

NUTTY FUDGE PIE

2 tablespoons cooking oil	1 cup tiny marshmallows
¾ cup whole pecans	1 cup evaporated milk
Salt	Salt
1 cup semi-sweet chocolate pieces	1 quart vanilla ice cream, softened
	Chocolate Crumb Crust

Place oil in shallow baking pan. Stir in pecans. Bake in 350° oven until toasted, 12 to 15 minutes. Stir occasionally. Drain on paper toweling. Sprinkle with salt.

Combine chocolate, marshmallows, milk and dash salt in saucepan. Cook over medium heat, stirring constantly, until thick. Cool.

Spread half of ice cream in Chocolate Crumb Crust. Pour half of chocolate sauce over ice cream. Spread remaining ice cream over chocolate. Top with remaining sauce. Sprinkle with pecans. Freeze.

Chocolate Crumb Crust: Combine 1½ cup chocolate wafer crumbs and ¼ cup melted butter or margarine. Press into a 9-inch pie plate. Bake in 350° oven 10 minutes. Cool. (Vanilla wafers may be substituted, if desired.)

MUD PIE

22 chocolate sandwich cookies, chopped fine
6 tablespoons melted butter
1 quart chocolate ice cream

2 tablespoons instant decaffeinated coffee
2 tablespoons brandy
2 tablespoons coffee-flavored liqueur
1 cup heavy cream, whipped

Mix cookie crumbs and butter. Press into 9-inch pie plate. Freeze. Whip softened ice cream with instant coffee, brandy and coffee-flavored liqueur. Fold in 4 tablespoons whipped cream. Pour into frozen crust. Freeze. Before serving, top with whipped cream. Cut with hot knife. Serve with cherry on each slice, if desired. Makes 6 to 8 servings.

Alternate: for slightly milder flavor, use 1 pint chocolate ice cream and 1 pint vanilla ice cream.

STRAWBERRY CREAM CHEESE PIE

A luscious, fresh strawberry pie.

1 8-ounce package cream cheese
½ cup sour cream
Unbaked 9-inch graham cracker crust
3 pints strawberries

2¼ cups sugar plus 2 tablespoons
3 tablespoons cornstarch
1/8 teaspoon vanilla

Blend the cream cheese with ¼ cup sour cream. Measure ½ cup and spread it on the bottom of the chilled pie shell. Hull 2 pints of strawberries and sprinkle with 1½ cups of sugar; set aside. Crush 1 pint of hulled strawberries, sprinkle with ¾ cup sugar and let stand until juicy. Rub through a sieve. Measure the juice and add water to make 1½ cups. Mix in the cornstarch and heat and stir until thick. Cool. Pour a thin layer of the sauce into the shell and add the remaining berries, drained. Top with remaining sauce and chill. Add remaining sugar, sour cream and vanilla to the rest of the cream cheese. Chill and garnish the pie with this mixture. Makes 6 to 8 servings.

SOUR CREAM PEACH PIE

The name alone conjures up the picture of a summer day, a pitcher of iced tea, and this luscious dessert.

1 9-inch pie shell, baked	½ teaspoon cinnamon
5 cups sliced fresh peaches	¼ teaspoon nutmeg
½ cup packed brown sugar	Dash salt
1 tablespoon cornstarch	1½ cups sour cream

Toss peaches with brown sugar, cornstarch, cinnamon, nutmeg and a dash of salt. Turn into baked pie crust. Pour sour cream over fruit. Cover edges with foil. Bake in 400° oven for 25 minutes, or until crust is golden. Serve hot or cold topped with a dollop of sour cream. Makes 6 servings.

LEMON MERINGUE PIE

Pretty enough to eat with its puffs of meringue.

1 9-inch baked pie shell	2 tablespoons butter
1⅓ cups sugar	½ cup fresh lemon juice
½ cup cornstarch	1 tablespoon grated lemon peel
¼ teaspoon salt	¼ teaspoon cream of tartar
1¾ cup water	½ cup sugar
4 eggs, separated	

Bake pie shell and cool. Combine in saucepan the sugar, cornstarch and salt. Gradually add the water. Cook over medium heat, stirring constantly until it comes to a boil and boil for 1 minute. Beat egg yolks slightly in a bowl and slowly add ½ cup of the hot mixture. Mix and gradually add more hot mixture until all danger of curdling is past. Return to pan and cook 2 minutes over low heat, stirring constantly. Remove from heat. Add the butter, lemon juice and grated lemon peel. Pour into pie shell and cool for 3 hours.

Meringue: Beat the egg whites and cream of tartar until foamy and double in size. Slowly add the sugar and beat until stiff. Pile 6 or 7 good sized puffs onto a greased and floured cookie sheet. Bake at 425° for 3 to 5 minutes, until lightly browned. Lift off cookie sheet and arrange on top of pie.

Date Nut Rolls

¼ pound margarine
1-8 ounce package pitted dates
1 cup chopped nuts
1 cup sugar

Pinch salt
1 teaspoon vanilla
1½ cups crisp rice cereal
Confectioners' sugar

Melt margarine in large saucepan. Add dates, nuts, sugar and salt. Cook for 8 minutes over low heat.

Remove from heat; add vanilla and cereal. Cool until mixture can be worked with hands.

Shape into finger-sized rolls or walnut-sized balls. Roll in confectioners' sugar. Yields 3-3½ dozen.

With best wishes, Rosalynn Carter

LAYERED PUMPKIN DESERT

Crust:
24 graham crackers, crushed
⅓ cup sugar
½ cup butter
First Layer:
2 eggs, beaten
¾ cup sugar
8 ounce cream cheese
1 teaspoon vanilla
Second Layer:
2 cups pumpkin

3 egg yolks
½ cup sugar
½ cup milk
½ teaspoon salt
1 tablespoon cinnamon
½ teaspoon allspice
½ teaspoon nutmeg
1 envelope plain gelatin
¼ cup cold water
3 egg whites
¼ cup sugar

Mix crust ingredients and press into 13x9x2-inch pan. Mix first layer and pour over crust. Bake 20 minutes at 350°. Cool. Meanwhile, combine next eight ingredients and cook, stirring, until mixture thickens. Remove from heat and add gelatin, which has been dissolved in cold water. Cool. Beat egg whites and ¼ cup sugar, then fold into cooled pumpkin mixture. Pour over cooled, baked crust. Refrigerate several hours. Serve with whipped cream.

OATMEAL CRISPS

These will wait in the refrigerator to be baked at a moment's notice.

1 cup butter or margarine	1½ cups all-purpose flour
1 cup brown sugar, packed	1 teaspoon baking soda
1 cup granulated sugar	1 teaspoon salt
2 eggs, beaten	3 cups oatmeal
	1 teaspoon vanilla

Cream butter and sugars. Add eggs and beat well. Add dry ingredients. Form into 2 or 3 long rolls and wrap in waxed paper. Chill several hours or several days. (Can also be frozen.) Cut ¼-inch slices and bake on ungreased baking sheet in 350° oven for about 12 minutes. Makes 5 dozen.

CANDY CANE COOKIES

Pretty on a mixed tray or alone on a plate with a dish of ice cream.

1 cup shortening (half butter)	1½ teaspoons almond extract
1 cup sifted confectioners' sugar	1 teaspoon vanilla
	2½ cups all-purpose flour
1 egg	1 teaspoon salt
	Several drops red food coloring

Mix thoroughly shortening, sugar, egg and flavorings. Sift flour and salt together and stir in. Divide dough in half and tint half of dough pink by mixing in as much red food coloring as desired. Chill all dough thoroughly.

Pinch off walnut-sized balls of dough and roll between hands till pencil-slim. Cut off even lengths and twist one pink and one white strand lightly together, curving at top to form crook of cane. Bake on greased baking sheet in 375° oven 9 minutes. Makes 4 dozen.

CRACKED SUGAR COOKIES

2 cups sugar	Dash salt
½ cup butter, softened	1 teaspoon soda
½ cup vegetable shortening	1 teaspoon cream of tartar
3 egg yolks	1 teaspoon vanilla or lemon
2 cups flour	extract
	Granulated sugar

Cream sugar, butter and shortening. Add egg yolks and continue beating. Sift dry ingredients and stir into creamed mixture, then add flavoring. Roll into balls about the size of a walnut. Roll in granulated sugar. Place on ungreased cookie sheet and bake in 300° oven about 15 minutes. These are prettiest if not brown. Makes about 3 dozen.

CHOCOLATE CRINKLES

A chocolate lover's delight. Mix up the night before and bake in the morning. Dough keeps for several days in refrigerator. Pretty enough for your tea table.

½ cup vegetable oil	2 teaspoon vanilla
4 squares unsweetened	2 cups all-purpose flour
chocolate, melted	2 teaspoons baking powder
2 cups granulated sugar	½ teaspoon salt
4 eggs	1 cup confectioners' sugar

Mix oil, chocolate, and granulated sugar. Blend in one egg at a time until well mixed. Add vanilla. Measure flour by dipping method or by sifting. Stir flour, baking powder, and salt into oil mixture. Chill several hours or overnight.

Heat oven to 350°. Drop teaspoonfuls of dough into confectioners' sugar. Roll in sugar; shape into balls. Place about 2 inches apart on greased baking sheet. Bake 10 to 12 minutes. Do not overbake. Makes about 6 dozen cookies.

FROSTED CASHEW COOKIES

½ cup butter or margarine	¾ teaspoon baking soda
1 cup brown sugar, packed	½ teaspoon cinnamon
1 egg	¼ teaspoon mace
½ teaspoon vanilla	¼ teaspoon salt
2 cups sifted all-purpose flour	⅓ cup sour cream
¾ teaspoon baking powder	1 cup coarsely chopped salted cashew nuts

Cream together butter and sugar. Add egg and vanilla and beat until light and fluffy. Sift together dry ingredients and add to creamed mixture alternately with sour cream. Stir in nuts. Drop by teaspoonfuls on greased cookie sheet 2 inches apart. Bake in 400° oven for 8 to 10 minutes. Remove from sheet at once and cool. Frost with Brown Butter Frosting. Makes 4 dozen.

Brown Butter Frosting: Heat and stir 3 tablespoons butter until browned. Slowly beat in 2 cups confectioners' sugar, 2 tablespoons milk and 1 teaspoon vanilla.

MINTED CHOCOLATE FUDGE

1 cup light cream	¼ cup green creme de menthe
2 cups sugar	2 tablespoons butter
4 ounces unsweetened chocolate	1 cup chopped nuts
¼ cup honey	¼ cup blanched grated Pistachio nuts (optional)

Bring the cream to boiling point with the sugar. Stir until sugar is dissolved. Melt the chocolate over boiling water. Stir chocolate into cream and sugar mixture and add the honey and creme de menthe. Cook to soft ball stage (240°). Add the butter and remove from heat. Let stand until lukewarm, then beat until creamy. Add the chopped nuts; pour into a buttered pan and dust with pistachio nuts, if desired. Cool in refrigerator. When firm, cut into squares.

A year or so after Grover Hubbell's death in 1956, his widow Anna moved out of Terrace Hill and the house was closed.

Terrace Hill was formally presented as a gift to the state of Iowa on August 24, 1971, at a ceremony outside the house on the south lawn. Four generations of the Hubbell family—including Anna Hubbell, the last occupant—watched as James W. Hubbell, Jr., gave the keys to Iowa Governor Robert D. Ray.

POTATO CHIP COOKIES

A delightfully crunchy, not-too-sweet cookie the whole family will enjoy.

1 pound butter or margarine	2 cups crushed potato chips
1 cup sugar	1 cup chopped pecans
3 cups sifted all-purpose	1 teaspoon vanilla
flour	Confectioners' sugar

Cream butter. Add sugar and beat until light and fluffy. Stir in flour. Mix well.

Stir in potato chips, nuts and vanilla. Drop by teaspoonfuls on ungreased cookie sheet. Bake in 325° oven 20 minutes. Cool; sprinkle with confectioners' sugar. Makes 7 dozen.

LAYERED COOKIE

A favorite of the Ray family

½ cup butter or margarine,
     melted
1 cup quick-cooking oats
½ cup brown sugar, packed
1 cup flour

Mix all ingredients until crumbly and pat into a 13x9x2-inch baking dish. Bake at 375° for 10 minutes. Remove from oven and cool.

½ cup brown sugar, packed	1 teaspoon baking powder
2 eggs	¼ teaspoon salt
1 teaspoon vanilla	1 cup chopped nuts
2 tablespoons flour	7 ounces chopped Heath bars
	1 cup coconut

Beat sugar and eggs together. Add vanilla, flour, baking powder and salt. Add nuts, candy and coconut and mix thoroughly. Spread on baked shell. Bake in 350° oven for 20 minutes. Cool and cut into squares. Makes 35 1½-inch squares.

WALNUT LACE COOKIES

⅓ cup flour	1 cup brown sugar
½ teaspoon baking powder	1 egg, slightly beaten
1/8 teaspoon salt	1 cup chopped walnuts
¼ cup butter or margarine	

Sift together flour, baking powder and salt. Blend butter, brown sugar and sifted dry ingredients with pastry blender as for pie crust. Add egg and mix thoroughly. Stir in walnuts. Drop thin batter by half teaspoon about 2 inches apart on buttered teflon-lined cookie sheet. Bake at 350° 4 to 5 minutes. Let stand 2 or 3 minutes; remove to rack with spatula. Makes about 4 dozen.

LEMON LOVE NOTES

A light and lemony tea favorite.

1 cup all-purpose flour	2 tablespoons lemon juice
¼ cup confectioners' sugar	1 cup granulated sugar
½ cup butter or margarine, softened	1 tablespoon grated lemon peel
2 eggs	½ teaspoon baking powder
2 tablespoons flour	1 cup confectioners' sugar
	Lemon juice

Blend together 1 cup flour, ¼ cup confectioners' sugar and butter. Pat into 9x9x2-inch baking pan. Bake in 350° oven 15 minutes.

Beat eggs. Combine with 2 tablespoons flour, 2 tablespoons lemon juice, granulated sugar, lemon peel and baking powder. Pour over crust. Bake in 350° oven 25 minutes.

Combine 1 cup confectioners' sugar with just enough lemon juice to make a thin icing. Drizzle over cookies while still hot. Spread carefully. Cut into small squares while warm. Chill well. Makes 81 1-inch squares.

PUMPKIN BARS

2 cups sugar	2 teaspoons baking powder
4 eggs	2 teaspoons ground cinnamon
1 16-ounce can pumpkin	1 teaspoon baking soda
1 cup salad oil	$\frac{1}{2}$ teaspoon salt
2 cups all-purpose flour	$\frac{1}{2}$ teaspoon ground nutmeg
	$\frac{1}{2}$ teaspoon ground cloves

Mix sugar, eggs, pumpkin and salad oil. Sift together dry ingredients and stir into pumpkin mixture. Pour into greased and floured 15x10x1-inch pan. Bake in 350° oven 25 to 30 minutes. Cool and frost with Cream Cheese Frosting. Makes about 6 dozen 2x1-inch bars.

Cream Cheese Frosting: Blend together 1 3-ounce package softened cream cheese, 3 tablespoons soft butter or margerine, 1½ cups confectioners' sugar and 1 tablespoon half and half or cream.

MOIST BROWNIES

Very easy and very moist, this will be your reliable brownie recipe.

4 1-ounce squares semi-sweet chocolate	4 whole eggs
	Dash salt
1 cup butter or margarine	1½ cups all-purpose flour
2 cups sugar	2 teaspoons vanilla

In saucepan, melt together chocolate and butter over low heat. Add remaining ingredients and mix well. Spread in greased 13x9x2-inch pan. Bake in 350° oven 30 minutes. Do not overbake. Frost if desired. Makes 24.

PEANUT BUTTER CUPS

1 cup creamy peanut butter	$\frac{1}{4}$ cup margarine
$\frac{1}{2}$ pound powdered sugar	Approximately 1 pound dipping chocolate

Blend first three ingredients in food processor. Chill slightly, and with hands, roll in balls the size of walnuts. Melt chocolate. Place 1 teaspoon chocolate in bottom of individual paper candy cups. Drop in peanut butter balls and cover with more melted chocolate. Let stand until firm.

PRALINES

1 pound light brown sugar	1 tablespoon butter
1/8 teaspoon salt	2 cups pecan halves
¾ cup evaporated milk	

Mix the brown sugar, salt and evaporated milk in a medium size, heavy saucepan. Cook and stir over low leat until sugar is dissolved. Add the butter and pecans and cook over medium heat to soft ball stage, 234° to 238°, stirring constantly. Remove from heat and let cool 5 minutes. Stir rapidly until mixture begins to thicken and coat pecans lightly. Drop quickly from teaspoon on lightly buttered baking sheet. If candy becomes too stiff stir in a few drops of hot water. For large candies, drop candy from tablespoon. Makes 44 small or about 20 large candies.

PEANUT BRITTLE

2 cups sugar	2 teaspoons baking soda
1 cup white corn syrup	2 cups raw peanuts
½ cup water	1 tablespoon butter
¼ teaspoon salt	1 teaspoon vanilla

Cook first 4 ingredients to hard ball stage, then add peanuts and butter and cook until light brown, 290°, stirring constantly. Remove from heat and add soda and vanilla. Mix quickly and pour on large cookie sheet, cool and break into pieces.

POPCORN BALLS

A favorite of the Ray family.

3 quarts salted popcorn	¼ cup butter or margarine
1 cup sugar	Pinch of salt
⅓ cup light corn syrup	¾ teaspoon vanilla
⅓ cup water	

Pop corn. Put sugar, syrup, water, butter and salt in large saucepan and stir until sugar dissolves. Then boil until it forms a hard ball in cold water or the temperature reaches 250° to 290° on a candy thermometer. Remove from heat and stir in vanilla. Add the popcorn and form into balls.

BUCKEYES

These candies look like the real thing and are sure to cause comment at any gathering.

2 18-ounce jars creamy peanut butter, room temperature
1 pound butter or margarine, softened
3 pounds confectioners' sugar
2 12-ounce packages chocolate chips
2 ounces paraffin

Mix peanut butter, butter and sugar together until smooth texture develops. Form into small balls the size of buckeyes. Refrigerate 2 to 3 hours. Slowly melt chocolate chips and paraffin together in top of double boiler. Using a toothpick, dip the cold buckeyes into the chocolate, leaving the top uncovered. Let dry on waxed paper. Makes about 166 candies. Paraffin may be omitted but candies need to be refrigerated. These may be frozen.

CARAMELS

Choose dry weather to make these caramels and you will be delighted with the results.

½ cup butter
1 cup sugar
¾ cup light corn syrup
⅔ cup evaporated milk
1 teaspoon vanilla

Cook butter, sugar and syrup until it carmelizes, about 5 minutes. Slowly add the evaporated milk and stir in the vanilla. Cook to the soft ball stage 234° to 238°. Pour in a buttered 9x9x2 -inch pan and let set. Cut in small pieces and wrap each piece in waxed paper.

IOWA'S
FIRST
FAMILY

Governor Robert D. Ray, his wife Billie and daughters Randi, Lu Ann and Vicki are the first family to reside at Terrace Hill since it has been the property of the state. The family's quarters on the third floor were the first to be remodeled and refurbished. The Governor and Billie have taken a great interest in the restoration of the remainder of the house.

The third floor quarters, a living room, dining room, kitchen and four bedrooms, are reached by elevator from the private side entrance of the house and afford privacy and a comfortable atmosphere for family life and also for hosting small groups.

The first floor parlors and dining room are partially restored and refurnished. They are open for viewing by the public and are also used for official functions on special occasions. The second floor, when restored, will contain several small dining-meeting rooms, a guest suite for visitors and offices for the Governor and spouse. A new fully-equipped kitchen is in the basement so that food for official occasions can be prepared and served on the premises.

Terrace Hill allows the Rays to lead both private and public lives, and sometimes the two blend together. In private life the Governor enjoys reading, photography and tennis and has been known to raid the refrigerator for his favorite treat, a dish of ice cream. Billie pursues her interests in tennis and needlepoint when she finds the time. The girls have run the gamut of high school and college activities, jobs and travel and accept the demands on their time, and those of their parents, that are imposed by public service.

The following pages contain some family pictures, favorite recipes, and a photo collection of various celebrities who have been a part of the Rays' public life.

Pictured on the second floor landing with the magnificent stained glass window behind them are Governor and Mrs. Robert D. Ray and daughters Vicki, Lu Ann and Randi. The family dog is Heini.

The family living room is bright and warm in a more comfortable style than the formal rooms below.

The family dining room is used by the family and their friends regularly and often hosts state visitors as well.

Colorful Roman shades at the rounded third-floor windows mark the only reminder that this modern kitchen is at Terrace Hill. Mattie Cutwright prepares meals and party dishes for the Rays.

The master bedroom.

Vicki's bedroom, where Lillian Carter stayed in November, 1977.

The Rays are often invited to ride in parades throughout Iowa.

Skiing is an activity the entire family enjoys.

Ray Family Album

Favorite Ray Family Recipes

LU'S SUMMER SAUSAGE

2   pounds lean ground beef
1   cup water
2   tablespoons liquid smoke

2   tablespoons curing salt
¼   teaspoon onion powder
¼   teaspoon garlic powder

Mix all ingredients well and form in two long loaves, about 3 inches in diameter. Wrap in foil, shiny side to meat. Place in baking dish and refrigerate 24 hours. Bake 90 minutes in 350° oven. (Bake in dish to keep oven clean.) When cool, slice and serve with cocktail bread. Store in refrigerator.

SLUSHY PUNCH

3   small packages lime jello
9   cups boiling water
4   cups sugar
4   cups warm water
1   16-ounce bottle lemon
     juice

2   46-ounce cans pineapple
     juice
2   quarts gingerale
4   bananas, mashed
1   18-ounce can crushed
     pineapple

Dissolve jello in boiling water. Mix sugar in warm water and bring to boil, add to jello mixture and cool. When cool add lemon juice and pineapple juice, mixing well. Add mashed bananas and the crushed pineapple.

Fill 4 ½-gallon milk cartons with the mixture and freeze solid. Make a day ahead. Before serving remove cartons and let thaw. Pour in punch bowl and add gingerale. Makes 50 servings.

CHEESEY CHOWDER

1 cup chopped potatoes	3 cups chicken broth
½ cup chopped carrots	Dash white pepper
½ cup chopped celery	2 cups milk
½ cup chopped onion	½ cup all-purpose flour
½ cup chopped green pepper	3 cups (12 ounces) shredded
4 tablespoons butter or	sharp process American
margarine	cheese
	1 tablespoon snipped parsley

In a Dutch oven, cook potatoes, carrots, celery, onion and green pepper in butter until tender, but not brown. Add chicken broth and pepper. Cover and simmer 30 minutes. Blend milk into flour. Add to chowder with cheese and parsley. Cook and stir until thickened and bubbly. Makes 7 to 8 servings.

HEALTH BREAD

2 envelopes dry yeast	2 cups reconstituted nonfat
1 cup lukewarm water	dry milk
⅓ cup sugar or ⅓ cup honey	⅓ cup light or dark molasses
⅓ cup vegetable shortening	1 cup wheat germ
3 teaspoons salt	3 cups whole wheat flour
2 eggs	6 cups (about) white flour

Dissolve yeast in lukewarm water. Stir in sugar or honey, shortening, salt, milk and molasses. Beat in eggs, wheat germ and whole wheat flour. The dough will be heavy enough now that the white flour will have to be added by hand. Make a stiff dough, kneading until elastic.

Let rise until double in bulk. Shape into rolls or loaves and let rise again. Bake in a 375° oven 40 to 45 minutes—less for rolls or small loaves. Makes 3 loaves in 8½x4½x3-inch pans.

BAR-B-Q RIBS

4 pounds spare ribs	¼ cup vinegar
1 teaspoon salt	¼ cup water
½ teaspoon pepper	3 teaspoons sugar
6 or 8 leaves from celery ribs	½ teaspoon cinnamon
1 cup catsup	

Season ribs with salt and pepper and brown in dutch oven or covered skillet in a little fat. Cover with celery leaves. In a saucepan, combine catsup, vinegar, water, sugar and cinnamon. Bring to boil over medium heat, then pour over ribs and celery leaves. Cover and bake in a 350° oven 1½ hours, basting every 15 minutes.

TOMATO BEEF LOAF

2 pounds ground beef	1¾ cups dry bread crumbs
¾ cup chopped onion	1 16-ounce can tomatoes
1 stalk celery, chopped	1 6-ounce can tomato paste
1 scant teaspoon salt	2 slightly beaten eggs
1/8 teaspoon pepper	½ cup chopped green pepper

Saute onions and celery in butter until tender. Mix all ingredients thoroughly, except eggs and half of tomato paste. Add eggs gently. Place in 13x9x2-inch glass baking dish. Spread remainder of tomato paste over top (add some catsup if needed) and dot with chopped green pepper. Bake in 350° oven for 1½ hours. Cut in squares and serve.

VEGETABLE MEDLEY

Excellent choice to make in advance of your party and refrigerate. Allow 10 more minutes cooking time.

2 **10-ounce packages chopped broccoli**	2 **10¾-ounce cans condensed cream of mushroom soup**
1 **16-ounce can sliced carrots, drained**	1 **cup shredded sharp process American cheese**
1 **16-ounce can lima beans, drained**	1 **8-ounce can water chestnuts, drained and sliced**
1 **teaspoon prepared mustard**	1 **4-ounce can mushroom stems and pieces, drained**
2 **teaspoons salt**	**Toasted, slivered almonds**
Dash pepper	
1 **tablespoon minced onion**	

Cook broccoli in boiling, salted water until just tender; drain well. Stir together with remaining ingredients except almonds. Spoon into 13x9x2-inch baking dish. Sprinkle nuts over top. Bake in 350° oven 35 to 40 minutes. Makes 16 servings.

BAKED PINEAPPLE

A sweet accompaniment for pork.

¼ **cup sugar**	1 **29½-ounce can crushed pineapple**
3 **tablespoons flour**	¼ **to ½ pound grated Cheddar cheese**
½ **teaspoon salt**	**Buttered crumbs**

Mix first three ingredients and add the pineapple and cheese. Pour into buttered 1½-quart casserole. Top with buttered crumbs. Bake in 350° oven for 40 minutes. Makes 8 to 10 servings.

The Governor enjoying a colossal portion of his favorite treat—ice cream.

CREAMY VANILLA ICE CREAM

An unusually delicious ice cream. Add strawberries or peaches in season, if you like.

2	cups sugar	6	eggs beaten
2	tablespoons flour	1	15-ounce can evaporated milk
½	teaspoon salt	1	quart half and half
4	cups milk	½	pint whipping cream
		2	teaspoons vanilla

Mix sugar, flour, salt and milk. Cook and stir until slightly warm; add eggs. Cook over medium heat, stirring constantly, until mixture coats spoon (about 5 minutes). Pour half of mixture into blender and add half of the following: evaporated milk, half and half, whipping cream and vanilla. Blend. Pour into 1-gallon freezer container. Repeat blending with remainder of ingredients. Freeze. Makes 1 gallon.

HOMEMADE VANILLA ICE CREAM

A basic back porch recipe that makes any gathering a special occasion.

4 eggs	3½ tablespoons vanilla
1 cup sugar	1 cup light corn syrup
1 cup whipping cream	Dash salt
1 pint half and half	1½ to 2 quarts milk

Beat eggs until frothy. Add sugar and beat well. Add cream, half and half, vanilla, corn syrup and salt and beat. Pour into hand or electric ice cream freezer. Add milk up to 4 or 5 inches from top. Freeze.

For Lemon Ice Cream: Reduce vanilla to 1 tablespoon and add 2 teaspoons lemon flavoring.

BANANA CARAMEL NUT ICE CREAM

2¼ cups packed brown sugar	6¾ cups half and half
6 tablespoons butter or margarine	¾ cup chopped English walnuts
3 cups mashed bananas	3 tablespoons vanilla

Melt brown sugar and butter together, stirring until blended. Add half and half, bananas, walnuts, and vanilla. Place in a 1 gallon ice cream freezer. Freeze.

THREE-FRUIT SHERBET

Juice of 7 lemons	6 bananas, mashed
Juice of 6 oranges	4 to 5 cups sugar
	Milk

Combine lemon and orange juice. Blend a little juice into bananas, beating until smooth. Stir in sugar. Place in 1 gallon ice cream freezer can. Add enough milk to make can ⅔ full. Freeze.

APPLE CAKE WITH BUTTER SAUCE

Sauce will keep up to two weeks in refrigerator in tight container, if you wish to freeze part of the cake.

2	cups sugar	2 teaspoons ground cinnamon
½	cup butter or margarine, softened	1 teaspoon ground nutmeg
2	eggs	1 teaspoon salt
2	cups all-purpose flour	4 cups finely chopped pared apples
1	teaspoon baking soda	1 cup chopped nuts

Cream together sugar and butter. Add eggs and beat until light and fluffy. Sift together dry ingredients. By hand, stir in dry ingredients. Fold in apples and nuts. Place in greased 13x9x2-inch baking pan. Bake in 350° oven 15 minutes; reduce heat to 300° and bake 45 minutes. Serve warm or cold with Butter Sauce. Makes 18 servings.

Butter Sauce: Combine 1 cup sugar, ¼ cup half and half, and ½ cup butter over low heat, stirring constantly, until sugar dissolves. Remove from heat and add 1 teaspoon vanilla. Serve warm.

CARAMEL CORN

A festive treat for party-goers of all ages.

2	cups brown sugar	1 teaspoon salt
1	cup butter or margarine	1 teaspoon baking-soda
½	cup white corn syrup	6 quarts popped corn

Cook brown sugar, butter, syrup and salt for 5 minutes. Remove from heat and add soda. Pour over popped corn. Spread on greased cookie sheet and place in 200° oven for 1 hour, stirring every 15 minutes.

VICKI'S TOFFEE CANDY

½	pound butter	1 teaspoon vanilla
1	cup sugar	¾ cup chopped nuts
3	tablespoons water	6 sweet chocolate candy bars

Cook butter, sugar, water and vanilla until brown; about 10 minutes. Add ½ cup of chopped nuts. Pour on greased cookie sheet. Cover with the candy bars while warm and spread over surface. Sprinkle with the remaining nuts. Let cool and break into pieces.

RANDI'S COOKIES

You will want to keep the cookie jar stocked with these nourishing treats.

1 cup shortening	1 teaspoon baking powder
1 cup sugar	½ teaspoon salt
1 cup brown sugar, packed	1 cup quick cooking oatmeal
2 eggs	1 cup each rice crispies
1 teaspoon vanilla	and cornflakes
2 cups all purpose flour	1 cup chopped nuts
1 teaspoon baking soda	

Cream shortening and sugars and beat in eggs and vanilla. Sift flour, soda, baking powder, salt and add oatmeal. Then add cereals and nuts. May also add 1 cup raisins or snipped dates. This is a heavy batter and you will need to use your hands to work in all these ingredients. Drop by teaspoonful onto oiled cooky sheets and bake at 350° for 10 to 12 minutes. Let stand a minute before removing from sheets. Makes about 9 dozen cookies.

L'ABRICOT ET AMANDE DESSERT

1½ cups crushed vanilla wafers	½ gallon vanilla ice cream
⅓ cup melted butter	20 ounce jar apricot jam
⅔ cup toasted almonds	3 tablespoons orange flavored liqueur
1 teaspoon almond flavoring	

Mix the first 4 ingredients together, reserving ⅓ cup for topping. Using a 9x13-inch pan, press ½ mixture in bottom firmly. Add 1 quart ice cream. Put in freezer to refreeze ice cream. When firm, coat with about 10 ounces of apricot jam mixed with liqueur. Repeat layers and top with the remaining crumb mixture. Put in freezer. Cut in squares or serve in sherbet glasses and top with a cherry. Serves 12.

A formal evening out is not infrequent for the Rays, both in Des Moines and in other cities where they are on official visits. This picture was taken before dinner at a Governors' Conference in Oklahoma City.

Dinner in the White House Dining Room in 1977. Left to right are: President Jimmy Carter, Mrs. Reuben Askew, Governor Ray, Mrs. Cecil Andrus, Governor William Milliken, Mrs. Ray, Mrs. Milliken, Governor Reuben Askew and Mrs. Carter.

The Rays are greeted by President and Mrs. Gerald R. Ford, 1976.

President and Mrs. Ronald Reagan greet Governor and Mrs. Robert Ray at the White House in February, 1981.

Governor Ray, Nancy Reagan and Mrs. Ray having coffee after dinner at the White House in 1981.

President Ronald Reagan and Mrs. Robert Ray at White House dinner January 1981

President Ronald Reagan, Governor James B. Hunt, Jr., Governor Robert D. Ray, Governor John V. Evans, in conversation prior to breakfast at the White House.

First official house guest of the Governor's at Terrace Hill was "Miss Lillian" Carter, who joined Mrs. Ray and the Des Moines residents participating in the first Friendship force Exchange from Iowa to Dublin, Ireland.

Prince Faisal of Saudi Arabia takes time from official duties to visit the Rays' kitchen.

Governor Robert D. Ray, Secretary Henry Kissinger.

Governor Robert D. Ray, Vice-President Nelson Rockefeller.

The family hosts Ambassador Shirley Temple Black.

Governor Robert D. Ray, John Tone, then Governor Ronald Reagan.

Mrs. Dwight D. Eisenhower accepts a citizenship award from Governor Ray as former Governor Robert Blue looks on.

Governor John Connally breakfasts in the family dining room.

A dance with Lawrence Welk.

President Tito of Yugoslavia.

ACKNOWLEDGMENTS

A TASTE OF TERRACE HILL

Chairman: Billie Ray
Assistant Chairman: Greta Kelso
Steering Committee:

Millie Haynie	Ginger Monson
Cynthia Henderson	Carol Newcomer
LaDonna Matthes	Stacy Polydoran
Betsy McCracken	Genie Wilson
	Sue Wilson

Special thanks to testers Patti Barrett, June Braunger, Pat Cownie, Marilynn Crist, Willa Hoak, Sue King, Jane La Mair, Norma Lock, Terri Lowe, Sue McBroom, Jan McGarvey, Joyce Middleton, Margie Nahnsen, Marilyn Smith, Karla Tillotson, and Ann Willer; and to photographers John Schultz and Dave Penney.

Thanks also to many other contributors—recipe providers, photographers, Hubbell family members, the Terrace Hill Society and other friends who gave assistance and encouragement.

HISTORICAL RESOURCES:
Goettsch, Scherrie and Weinberg, Steve, Terrace Hill, Des Moines, Wallace Homestead Book Co., 1978.
Mills, George S. Little Man With a Long Shadow, Des Moines The Trustees of the Frederick M. Hubbell Estate, 1955.

Terrace Hill sketch by Bill Wagner.

Second Edition: Design consultant and photography by Truepenny Studios, Inc. Duane Swensen, President.

Published by the Terrace Hill Society, a non-profit organization dedicated to the restoration and preservation of Terrace Hill.
Address: Terrace Hill Society
       State Treasurer's Office
       State Capitol
       Des Moines, Iowa 50319

INDEX

D

NEW RECIPES LISTED
ON NEXT PAGE

INDEX OF NEW RECIPES
SECOND EDITION